John Stockton: The Inspiring Story of One of Basketball's Greatest Point Guards

An Unauthorized Biography

By: Clayton Geoffreys

Table of Contents

Foreword

Whenever anyone is asked to name the greatest point guards of all time, it does not take long before John Stockton is mentioned. Throughout the majority of the 1980s and 1990s, John Stockton was one of the most productive point guards in the league. By the time he retired, Stockton averaged a career double-double, a feat often only accomplished by the all-time greats. While he was never able to win a NBA Championship, Stockton retired as one of the most respected guards to ever play the game. If you have a deep appreciation of pass-first point guards, there is no better story to learn than that of John Stockton. Thank you for purchasing *John Stockton: The Inspiring Story of One of Basketball's Greatest Point Guards*. In this unauthorized biography, we will learn John Stockton's incredible life story and impact on the game of basketball. Hope you enjoy and if you do, please do not forget to leave a review!

Also, check out my website at claytongeoffreys.com to join my exclusive list where I let you know about my latest books. To thank you for your purchase, you can go to my site to download a free copy of *33 Life Lessons: Success Principles, Career Advice & Habits of Successful People*. In the book, you'll learn from some of the greatest thought leaders of different industries on what it takes to become successful and how to live a great life.

Cheers,

Clayton Geoffreys

Visit me at www.claytongeoffreys.com

Introduction

It is often said that an NBA player's status as one of the all-time greats is determined by the number of championships he won during his playing days. Those considered great have won titles. Michael Jordan ended his career as a six-time champion. Bill Russell won 11 titles during the 60's. Despite all the battles he had with Russell, Wilt Chamberlain retired as a two-time NBA champion. Kareem Abdul-Jabbar spent a lifetime not only collecting points but also six NBA rings. Magic Johnson and Larry Bird combined for a total of eight championships during their rivalry years in the 80's. And in today's league, LeBron James is continuing to carve out his legacy as one of the players that could one day be the greatest of all time as he seeks out more NBA titles.

But what if those legendary players that did not have the pleasure of being called an NBA champion? Winning an NBA title was never easy no matter how good a player was because championships were always dependent on how the team played and of how tough the competition was. Some players won titles because of how completely dominant their team was during their peak years. And there were those that collected multiple championships during an era where the NBA was not at its most competitive.

Though the popular belief is that a championship defines a player's career, it is never truly a measure of how great the player was. Some superstars could not get over the hump because of the era and competitive environment they played in. One of those players is the Utah Jazz's legendary point guard, John Stockton.

John Stockton spent his entire NBA career as a player that reveled in seeing his teammates making baskets. It was as if the point guard position was made for him. He was a playmaker like no other. He became an All-Star by making sure his teammates had the best possible shots and looks. He played hard-nosed defense and provided the Jazz with a secondary or tertiary scoring punch because of how talented of a shooter he was. Stockton even revolutionized what is considered the most fundamental play in basketball.

Known as the master of the pick-and-roll, John Stockton was the initiator of what is arguably the best point guard and big man tandem in the history of basketball. While playing under legendary head coach Jerry Sloan, Stockton used his masterful abilities as a passer and playmaker to revolutionize the pick-and-roll together with fellow all-time great Karl Malone.

Together, the two wreaked havoc on the NBA with basketball's most fundamental play. Stockton's ability to handle and pass the ball was in complete sync with Malone's athleticism, power, and finishing skills. It was almost impossible to stop the two on the offensive end. The three words "Stockton to Malone" had become a common phrase in the NBA because of how effective Stockton was at finding his big man in the pick-and-roll.

Everybody knew that the screen was going to come and the pass was probably going to Karl Malone. However, John Stockton always found a way to make the pick-and-roll work because of how great of a passer and playmaker he was. He saw plays before they happened. He could find open teammates waiting in the wings for open shots when Malone was shut down. And if the pass was not available, he knew how to take matters into his own hands. While Malone was considered the Jazz's best player and most imposing figure, Stockton was the head of the snake. He was the vital cog that made the Utah Jazz machinery work. In many ways, he was what made the pick-and-roll offense work.

As the Jazz were headed into the 90's, John Stockton helped Utah become relevant and competitive in one of the NBA's toughest eras. The Utah Jazz became one of the most competitive teams during the 90's because of how Stockton orchestrated their pick-and-roll offense. But it was not until the latter half of the decade when the Jazz truly became one of the best teams of that era.

The Utah Jazz would win 64 games during the 1996-97 regular season and were one of the best teams in the entire league. Stockton was at the helm of the offense while Karl Malone was their MVP and best player. They dominated the Western Conference picture to power into the NBA Finals. They were arguably one of the best teams in the world and would have been title favorites in any other era. However, they ran up against one of the greatest teams in the history of the NBA.

The 1995-98 Chicago Bulls are considered one of the best teams in a three-year span. Leading that all-time great team was Michael Jordan, who is considered the greatest player in the history of the game. Against the Bulls, the Utah Jazz were helpless and lost the 1997 Finals in six games. The following year, Stockton and Malone led the Utah Jazz to the NBA Finals yet again only to fall to the Bulls once more in six games. Since then, John Stockton would never come closer to winning an NBA championship.

Playing 19 seasons in the league for the same franchise until he was 40 years old, John Stockton retired as a ten-time All-Star and the league's all-time leader in assists and steals. However, Stockton would never become an NBA champion. To his credit, a lot of the NBA's best players were unable to win a title during the 90's because of the Chicago Bull's dominance. John Stockton was one of those unfortunate greats that had to play during the era of Michael Jordan's peak.

Nevertheless, John Stockton's greatness and status as one of the best players to have ever played never diminished even though he failed to win a single championship. He is one of the NBA's best point guards and may perhaps be the greatest pure passer in the history of the league. And as the point guard that revolutionized the pick-and-roll, Stockton will forever be the first name mentioned in "Stockton to Malone," a phrase that has been mentioned thousands of times.

Chapter 1: Early Life and High School Career

Before he was dropping dimes and bouncing passes towards a streaking Karl Malone, John Houston Stockton was a scrawny baby boy born on March 26, 1962, in Spokane, Washington to Jack and Clementine Stockton. Named after his grandfather, a former NFL player back in the 1920's, there was reason to believe that John Stockton was going to grow up to be a great athlete. However, it was otherwise. But what John Stockton lacked in size and athleticism he made up for in grit and resiliency. Such grit and resiliency started with his father, Jack.

Jack Stockton spent much of his life as a hard worker in a place called Jack and Dan's, a tavern that he and his friend Dan Crowley bought in 1961. Formerly called Joey's Tavern, it was not until 1975 when Jack and Dan decided to change the name. It was through the bar that Jack and Clementine provided for John and his three other siblings. Business was great for the Stockton household, especially considering that they lived close to Gonzaga University.[i] The simple and hard-working life that Jack led helped his son John work just as hard for his career as a future basketball Hall-of-Famer.

John Stockton's early life had an easy routine. Living in Spokane, Washington, his life was limited to a small section of the city. School was merely a few blocks from his family's home. After school, he would then visit his dad at Jack and Dan's for a short break before indulging himself in a snack from across the street. And just a block away from Jack and Dan's was Gonzaga University, where John would routinely sneak in to play basketball with the bigger and older boys.[ii]

When John Stockton was not trying to sneak into Gonzaga, he was spending his free time hooping in the family's driveway. As his father recalled, John spent night and day playing basketball there and did not care whether it was raining or snowing. While Jack and Clementine's favorite player at that time was Bob Cousy, who was considered to be the best point guard in the history of the NBA at that point, played a little different.

John Stockton was in high school when Gus Williams played for the Seattle SuperSonics, which is now the Oklahoma City Thunder. Basketball was always big in the Northeast and especially in Seattle. Because of this, John Stockton played more like Gus Williams than Bob Cousy. He would even get to meet Williams in person when the Sonics met the Utah Jazz in an exhibition game in Spokane. Stockton, a high schooler back then, was a ball boy that game. It was the exposure to the NBA that day that made Stockton believe he would one day become an NBA player.[i]

But nobody outside of John himself believed he would one day become an NBA player. He had huge hands and feet, but that was about it. He was a scrawny little white kid that was not big or athletic enough to make it in a league dominated by faster and more explosive players. In some way, John Stockton's dreams were even bigger than his hands and feet were. But doubts never stopped him from working hard for that dream.

While playing for Gonzaga Prep, which was a mile away from home, John Stockton was a star after he moved on from St. Aloysius, the Gonzaga system's affiliated grade school. The 5'5" ninth grader was still waiting to grow as people around him thought he was still too small to make something of himself in the world of basketball. Ed Smith, his ninth-grade coach, thought that he was not only small but also not as quick as some of the players of his size and age. Physically, John Stockton was just one of the other normal kids. He was only good enough to start and become the fourth-best scorer in his ninth-grade team. Smith called the young Stockton "Midget," yet still hoped he would grow enough to make it to varsity in his senior year.[iii]

But size never stopped John Stockton from succeeding. Back in eighth grade at St. Aloysius, his coach Kerry Pickett had to rely on him when their best player fouled out. He was looking at an 85-pound scrawny kid and told him to be "The Man" of the team during that overtime period. Stockton did more than what he was expected to do and carried his team on his small shoulders to that overtime win.

But that was not grade school anymore, and John Stockton had to spend high school being compared to what the two other stars in Spokane could do. Ryne Sandberg was graceful and had baseball skills. Meanwhile, Mark Rypien, a point guard himself, was a powerful and athletic player given his inclination towards football. They were both bigger than Stockton, but the scrawny little kid had bigger dreams and aspirations.

John Stockton was able to make something of himself in his high school years by working harder than anyone else. He breathed basketball. Stockton played basketball in school, at the local YMCA, and also in other neighboring schools. He would even sneak in to play with older intramural college players at Gonzaga University. John Stockton was not afraid of the competition and one day becoming one of the best in the sport even though he was playing against bigger and older players.[iii]

John Stockton did not stop at that. He would go on to spend time at home to work on his game by climbing up a small stool and dribbling a basketball in the dark. He would tell his sister Stacy that he was not working on his game but was doing something he loved. And during off days, he would even call his ninth-grade coach to open the school's gym and bring his friends, who were 20 to 30 years old. But even when the older men were beating him, the 5'5" guard never backed down. Smith would describe John as a talented and gifted player like several other young kids of his age. But what he had that nobody else in the area had was a desire to become the best.[iii]

By sophomore year, John Stockton had begun growing. His feet grew to about 12.5", and he had developed the speed that would soon become one of his trademark abilities as a basketball player. But that was not what made him a great prep player. His high school coach Terry Irwin described him as a young boy with a rare intangible skill for his age. John Stockton never dwelled on mistakes or good plays but would rather focus on the next one. He was competitive and hardworking, but none of his on-court highlights and mistakes ever got to his head. That was what made him a high school star despite his lack of physical tools and athleticism.

By the time he became a senior, John Stockton had grown to his mature size. Measured at 6'1" and weighing 165 pounds, Stockton had the right size for an ordinary point guard at a time when the world was looking at a 6'9" point guard named Magic Johnson playing for the LA Lakers in his rookie season in the NBA. Though he was slender and scrawny, Stockton used the tools he had to his advantage.

Scouts began watching what John Stockton could do. The skinny boy was hitting soft shots from the floor and was able to contort and bend his body whenever he tried to score near the rim. He used all of that to his advantage while shooting 58% from the floor during his senior year. That was despite the fact that he was launching shots about 20 feet away from the basket and with defenders trying to stop him from draining his jumpers.

As good as Stockton had become in his senior year, it was the way he led Gonzaga Prep that led scouts to believe he had the makings of a college player. Nobody expected the Gonzaga Bullpups to perform well during the 1979-80 season. The players did not even have confidence in themselves. However, John Stockton's hardworking nature and ability to make plays for others led his teammates to believe that they could salvage what everyone thought was going to be a bad season for the program. In the end, the Pups would only lose three of their final 13 games to earn a third-place finish at the end of the season.[iv]

But John Stockton did not lead his team solely on the offensive end as the league's leading scorer. He was even more dangerous on the defensive end of the floor. Despite his lack of size, he had a knack for getting in his man's face and would almost always force his defensive assignment out of his comfort zone. He also led his high school league in steals after tallying 91 the entire season. That was on top of his offensive skills as the top scorer and second-leading assist man in the area.

John Stockton's role as a senior was a far cry from his job during his junior year. The Bullpups had several great scoring players during the 1978-79 season. Because of that, Stockton's role was to make passes and plays for those players as Gonzaga was on its way to winning the 1979 championship. But even though he had grown into an offensive force in his senior year, Stockton was still most excited when he was making plays for others.[iv]

By the end of the season, John Stockton had surpassed all expectations. He had broken a 14-year record after finishing with a new single-season record of 373 total points for the Gonzaga Prep Pups. Because of that, he was highly recruited by schools such as the University of Idaho and the University of Montana. However, he would choose to stay close to home and one block away from Jack and Dan's Tavern. He chose to play for Gonzaga University.

Chapter 2: College Career

When John Stockton decided to attend Gonzaga University, he became the third generation of his family to attend the program. His grandfather was considered the greatest football player to have ever come out of Gonzaga. Jack also finished his collegiate studies at Gonzaga. It was only going to be a matter of time until John would become arguably the best basketball player to come out of the school since he continued his journey through the Gonzaga program since he was in grade school.

But John Stockton was set to join a program that was not expected to succeed. The Gonzaga Bulldogs had only won 16 out of the 27 games they played during the 1979-80 season. And in conference play, they were only 8-8 under head coach Dan Fitzgerald, who had heavily recruited John Stockton. They were not expected to become a much better team during the 1980-81 season especially after losing three starters to graduation.

John Stockton did not have a lot to be proud of during his freshman year at a small school like Gonzaga. He was playing behind veterans and starters such as Don Baldwin and Tim Wagoner. He was a backup point guard that provided only nine minutes a night for the Bulldogs. He averaged only 3.1 points and 1.4 assists as a freshman just a year after going for 23.3

points when he was a senior at Gonzaga Prep. However, that did not stop him from working harder.

Dan Fitzgerald, who would later become the Bulldogs' athletic director, raved about John Stockton ever since he saw him back at Gonzaga Prep. He had seen how competitive and hard working John Stockton was up close when he was scouting him back in high school. He would even often say that size was Stockton's only discernable weakness because the Spokane product had worked hard enough to cover every weakness he had in his game. And it was that same fire that made him improve his game every year at Gonzaga University.

John Stockton's always believed that when you are not practicing, somebody else is. This was the same motto that got him striving for his best every season when he was at Gonzaga. He would spend every night knocking on then-assistant coach Joe Hillock's door every night to ask for the keys to the gym. He wanted to work on his game every single night. And after two weeks, Hillock finally gave in. He would give the keys to Stockton and told security personnel to let the young point guard in every night.

John Stockton, ever the skinny playmaker, worked out with weights to try to strengthen his upper body in the hopes that it would help him keep up with bigger guards out on the perimeter or up against the towers that protected the paint. However, it was how he worked his discipline as a point guard that ultimately made him a star for Gonzaga. He trained well on how to make proper decisions. He was steadily learning how to pass, when to pass, and who to pass to.[v] It was that work ethic which made him a great player and one of the favorite leaders in that underdog Gonzaga roster.

By the time he was a sophomore, he had become a starter but was far from their best player. He was their starting point guard, but possessions usually had to go through forward Bill Dunlap and veteran guard Tim Wagoner. Despite that, Stockton was the team's third-leading scorer and their best passer after averaging 11.2 points and five assists. But after finishing 19-8 during his freshman year, Stockton could not save the Bulldogs from another mediocre season. Gonzaga finished the 1981-82 season 15-12. They were merely 7-7 in conference play.

John Stockton's star started to rise during his junior year. Starting alongside upstart sophomore Bryce McPhee, who was a good scorer and capable playmaker, Stockton was the lead guard in a backcourt that could outrun and outscore any other duo in the conference. He had become Gonzaga's best player after once again improving from where he left off in his sophomore year. The Gonzaga junior guard would average 13.9 points, 6.8 assists, and 2.5 steals during the 1982-83 season. However, the Bulldogs had worsened once again. Gonzaga finished the season 13-14 and would lose seven of their 12 conference games.

During his senior year, John Stockton truly became a national sensation for Gonzaga University. Similar to when he was in high school, during his senior year, he began to grow into himself both as a player and leader. Stockton would average 20.9 points, 7.2 assists, and 3.9 steals that season. He would lead the West Coast Atlantic Conference in scoring, assists, and steals, and was also the first player in Gonzaga history to record 1,000 points and 500 assists in the same season. Stockton would also win the West Coast Athletic Conference MVP award for being the best player in his conference that season. He would effectively become the school's greatest product in its history as a mediocre basketball program at that time.

John Stockton would also prove himself as a capable leader. While leading an offense that loved to run the fastbreak, Stockton thrived as a scorer and passer in transition. He would help Gonzaga win 17 of their 28 games that season. Despite not making the NCAA Tournament yet again, that was the best record the Gonzaga Bulldogs were able to muster up in the last 17 years.

After a marvelous individual season for the Gonzaga University Bulldogs, John Stockton surprisingly made the cut in a pool of 20 players that would be chosen to represent the United States in the 1984 Olympics. Back then, only college players were allowed to play in the Olympics since legendary Indiana Hoosiers coach Bob Knight was selected to form the team. However, Stockton failed to make the team as Bob Knight chose to cut him and future NBA All-Stars Charles Barkley and Terry Porter, among others. As history would later reveal, Stockton would get a chance to represent his country not only once, but twice.

By the time June of 1984 came around, John Stockton had already moved on from his Olympic snub and the Gonzaga program. He had already graduated from the University he had stayed at ever since he was in grade school. A product of Gonzaga through and through, he was prepared to take the next step in his basketball career and was finally going to leave the small portion of Spokane's map he was so accustomed to ever since he was a young boy. He was finally ready to try his hand in the NBA.

Chapter 3: NBA Career

The Legendary Class of 1984, Getting Drafted

John Stockton was set to join a 1984 class of NBA hopefuls that was as loaded with talent as any other class in the history of the league. In retrospect, some may even point out that the class of 1984 was the greatest class in the history of the league because of the sheer amount of superstar talent it produced when compared to any other class that came before or after it.

At the head of the draft class was the seven-foot beast of a center named Hakeem Olajuwon. He was coming out of Houston as a third-year veteran and the best player of a group of young players affectionately called *Phi Slama Jama* that also included star wingman Clyde Drexler, who was drafted a year before. Olajuwon was a defensive beast that protected the paint better than anyone else did while providing great numbers himself on the offensive end. There was almost no doubting his status as the favorite for the top overall pick, which the Houston Rockets owned.

But Olajuwon was not the only all-time great player in that class. Another youngster that stood out just as well as Olajuwon did and would later stand above any other name in the history of basketball was Michael Jordan, the junior guard out of North Carolina. As early as his freshman year, Jordan had already made a name for himself by draining a midrange jump shot to secure the 1982 NCAA title over the Georgetown Hoyas. He would then spend the next two seasons under Dean Smith as a two-way force that had all the talent in the world.

Another all-time great talent that hoped to make a splash in that draft class was Auburn's undersized big man, Charles Barkley. Despite his lack of size at the power forward spot, Barkley was a hard worker inside the paint. His skill and athletic level at 260 pounds had everyone in the nation surprised with what the junior could do. Like Olajuwon and Jordan, Barkley would later forge himself a career worthy of the Hall of Fame.

Other notable names in that draft class were Kentucky senior Sam Bowie, North Carolina senior Sam Perkins, Arkansas guard Alvin Robertson, Providence big man Otis Thorpe, and Michigan State senior Kevin Willis. Robertson, Thorpe, and Willis were some of the many players that became All-Stars out of that draft class, but their accomplishments paled in comparison to what Olajuwon, Jordan, and Barkley did. But Hakeem, MJ, and Sir Charles were not the only all-time great names that came out of that class. There was one future NBA legend that nobody in the world thought had the makings of a star. That man was John Stockton.

At first glance, nobody would ever expect John Stockton to one day become an All-Star let alone an all-time great. Standing at 6'1" and barely even 170 pounds, Stockton was not entirely small concerning height but was a skinny point guard at a time when the rest of the league wanted to have a 6'9" playmaker dropping dimes with ease like Magic Johnson was doing at the time. And when compared to other point guards such as Maurice Cheeks and Isaiah Thomas, he was not even as quick or athletic despite the fact that he was a strong sprinter.

But what John Stockton lacked in his physical abilities he more than made up for with his sheer hard work and grit as a highly-skilled point guard. One of the many reasons why he was getting attention from all over the nation was that he could do a lot even as a small guard. The best part about it was that he had so much control over the things he could do.[vi]

Though he was not the biggest, fastest, or most athletic point guard, John Stockton could do a lot with his quickness. But what was most amazing about Stockton's quickness was that he had control over it. Despite moving as quickly as he did, he had good court judgment and never did anything out of control. It was with this control and quickness that John Stockton could score near the basket despite his apparent lack of size and vertical leaping ability.

It was also John Stockton's mindset as a pure point guard that got scouts looking his way. Back in the 80's, the NBA raved about big men because the league was dominated by centers and power forwards that ruled the paint. The 1984 NBA Draft was no different. Save for Michael Jordan, all of the top prospects were centers and forwards. It was a rare sight to see guards that could play well. It was an even more unusual sight to see a point guard that had a pure playmaker's mentality.

John Stockton was lauded for his ability to play the position at a high level. He made all the decisions that a point guard should. He knew when to pass, who to pass to, and how to pass. In every way, he seemed like he relished making plays for others more than scoring the ball himself though he also knew when it was necessary for him to score the ball. He was an unselfish player that wanted his teammates to succeed as much as he did. There were even some that would say Stockton was a throwback to the days of Dick McGuire, the legendary New York Knicks point guard of the 1950's, whose sole purpose was to make sure his teammates had the best available shot.

John Stockton also resembled Bob Cousy a lot because of his large hands. He may not have been a massive player, but his hands were big enough for an ideal point guard. What also made him similar to Cousy, the Boston Celtics' legendary point guard, was that he had a temperament of a top athlete. He may have looked soft because of his skinny frame and boyish looks, but deep inside him burned the heart of a competitor that seemed to have lived on the streets.[ii]

While John Stockton did indeed have his physical limitations, what was most impressive about his natural abilities was that he was a durable and tireless sprinter. His coaches would always let the team play fast when Stockton was on the floor because the point guard never got tired of running. He even became popular among the Olympic hopefuls of 1984 because of how amazingly low his resting pulse rate was. No matter how fast he was going, his heart rate never shot up too high. It was always at the level of a trained long-distance runner.[v]

It was no secret that John Stockton could run the floor well and go for hours on the offensive end without tiring out. However, what was equally impressive was that he was exerting the same effort on the offensive end as he was on defense. Stockton used his freakish stamina and lateral movement to perform at the highest level on the defensive end. He would hound his assignment, get into people's faces, and harass his man for steals. That was the reason why he was always one of the leaders in steals in every level of basketball he played at. And it was even said that he could stop a three-on-one fast break on his own because of his terrific anticipation and lateral movement.[vi]

While there was no doubting John Stockton's abilities and skills at the point guard position, he still was not on par with the top prospects of that draft class. One of the reasons why scouts did not think too highly of him, other than his lack of size, was because he played for a small program in one of the less-competitive conferences in the country. At that time, Gonzaga was not known for producing the best basketball prospects or for its competitiveness in its conference.

Because Gonzaga was not an entire competitive program, Stockton never got to compete against the best players nor did he have the best teammates. He hardly won half of his games in Gonzaga and failed to make it to the NCAA Tournament in his four-year stay with the university. Nevertheless, Stockton was as good of a leader and player as anyone in the history of the program because of how he led Gonzaga to their best record in 17 years.

As draft day was nearing, the consensus belief was that John Stockton was not a top prospect but was sure to be taken either late in the first round or early in the second round. Stockton did not think he was going to be picked high but also thought that he was going to be taken by a team from the Northeast, where he had lived all his life. The Portland Trailblazers and the Seattle SuperSonics were interested in him, and John Stockton thought he was going to play just a handful of hours away from his hometown.

When the draft got started, the expected came to fruition as the Houston Rockets drafted Houston product Hakeem Olajuwon with their top overall pick. Then, the Portland Trailblazers surprised everyone by choosing center Sam Bowie with the second overall pick over the talented and proven Michael Jordan. While Bowie was a capable player and one that could have been a star, he was injury-riddled and would spend the rest of his career sidelined with injuries.

Then, with the third overall pick, the Chicago Bulls made arguably the best choice in league history by drafting Michael Jordan. Jordan would later rise to instant stardom as a rookie and would win the Rookie of the Year award. MJ would forge a career full of individual and team awards to earn himself the pleasure of being called one of the greatest of all time if he was not the best player in league history.

Two picks later, the Philadelphia 76ers would take the burly and undersized Charles Barkley in the first round to pair him up with Moses Malone, who was making a name for himself as a great center on par with Kareem Abdul-Jabbar. Together, Barkley and Malone would form the NBA's best rebounding tandem in the frontcourt. Pretty soon after, Charles Barkley would become an MVP and one of the best players to ever play the power forward position. He was the third Hall of Fame player to come out of that 1984 draft class.

As the draft proceeded, players believed to have star potential had already been taken. Some of them were able to become All-Stars themselves but were not on par with Olajuwon, Jordan, or Barkley. It turned out that it would take until the 16th pick of the draft for someone, who would later forge a career just as worthy for the Hall of Fame as Hakeem, MJ, or Sir Charles, to be taken despite the fact that fans were puzzled by the choice. The Utah Jazz would draft John Stockton with that pick.

Utah Jazz general manager and coach Frank Layden surprised a lot of spectators and followers when he decided to take John Stockton with their prized first-round pick. The Gonzaga product was a strong prospect but was a small guard. The Jazz were already secured at the guard spot with Rickey Green and Darrell Griffith both playing in the backcourt. The consensus belief was that they needed a big man to help out on scoring since neither Mark Eaton nor Thurl Bailey had it covered. But they took Stockton anyway.

The Utah Jazz had plenty of reasons to take John Stockton despite how the rest of the world thought they needed someone bigger. Layden was impressed with how Stockton performed during the Olympic tryouts for Bob Knight's team. He saw how hardworking and talented the small point guard was. Then he was convinced that Stockton could be the point guard of the future for the Utah Jazz, especially considering that Rickey Green, their starting playmaker, was about to enter his 30's.

But when John Stockton was taken by the Jazz and introduced to the Utah fans, there was silence. At first, Stockton thought the fans were booing him. He thought they did not like him. However, it was different. The fans were not booing John Stockton. Instead, they were saying "who." None of the fans knew who he was. And even if they did, he was a small guard that probably was not the best fit for the team at a time when what they needed was a big man.

However, the Utah Jazz front office was confident in their pick. They knew that they had chosen a gem at the 16th overall pick in what is now considered to be arguably the best draft class in league history. All they needed to do was to be patient with John Stockton and to trust in what the young 22-year-old rookie point guard could do for the team on both ends of the floor because they knew how hard of a worker he was. As hardworking as he was, Stockton was perfect for the equally hard working people of Utah. It was that hardworking mentality that would soon turn him into one of the greatest point guards in league history.

Rookie Season

When John Stockton was drafted, there were not a lot of expectations on his slender shoulders. He was not expected to produce right away but was seen as a backup to guards Rickey Green and Darrell Griffith. Everyone expected him to be a second-string point guard because Green, a veteran playmaker, was already their starter at that position.

While Stockton may have had a lot of potential, Rickey Green was a proven and tested player for a fast-paced and high-scoring Utah Jazz. Green was always considered one of the fastest players in the NBA. At that point in the history of the league, he was even considered one of the top guards concerning pure quickness. Even Stockton's ability to sprint the floor paled in comparison to how quick Green was. His speed and ability to make plays complemented star scorer Adrian Dantley and hot-shooting off guard Darrell Griffith. Because Green was the better choice at that time, John Stockton was expected to play and learn more from him at the point guard position.

John Stockton's NBA debut was on October 26, 1984, against the Seattle SuperSonics, a team he had grown to love watching as a child in Spokane, Washington. In 17 minutes off the bench, Stockton had a respectable NBA debut for a backup point guard after finishing the game with four points, five assists, and two steals. A night later, he had a better performance after going for six points, six assists, and two steals in a loss to the Los Angeles Clippers.

One of John Stockton's early breakthrough performances as an NBA player was on November 7, when the Utah Jazz defeated the Golden State Warriors for their third win of the season. In only 21 efficient minutes off the bench, he showed his quality as a point guard with star potential after going for 13 points, ten assists, and three steals. That would be the first of what would become hundreds of double-doubles for John Stockton.

Three days later on November 10, John Stockton would show that he also had the skills of a quality shooter and scorer in a loss to the Denver Nuggets. While playing 19 minutes as a backup, he made 7 of his 11 field goal attempts to score 19 points. Back when the three-point shot was still a rarity, he hit one of his two attempts that night. At that point, those 19 points were his career and season highs.

On November 27, John Stockton would start for the very first time in his career. In his first career start, he would only score two points on a 1 out of 5 shooting clip but was able to record a new career-high of 12 assists. Three days later in his third career start, he had 14 points, 11 assists, and four steals for his second career double-double. The Jazz won that game against Denver. The next night, he had another double-double in a loss to the Nuggets. He had 13 points, 12 assists, and three steals. Over the course of those four starts for John Stockton, he averaged 9.3 points, 10.3 assists, and 2.8 steals.

After those four games, John Stockton would promptly return to the bench when Rickey Green returned to the lineup. He would fail to replicate the performances he had as a starter but was still effective as Green's backup point guard. On January 6, 1985, he even had a quality game in a win over the Houston Rockets. In 21 minutes of play, he finished with ten points, seven assists, and a new career-high of five steals. John Stockton would have a similar performance a month later on February 5. In that loss to the Portland Trailblazers, the rookie point guard had ten points, eight assists, and five steals to tie his career-high in that department.

After spending the next month playing off the bench as Green's backup, John Stockton would return to the starting lineup for one more night. Showing that he had the qualities of a starting playmaker, he would go on to record 14 points, 11 assists, and two steals in 43 minutes of action in a win over the Chicago Bulls led by eventual Rookie of the Year Michael Jordan.

On March 11, just when the season was about to end, John Stockton would have his fifth and final double-double of the regular season. In that win over the Portland Trailblazers, the rookie point guard out of Gonzaga would go for 14 points, 11 assists, and two steals. He did all of that in only 22 minutes of action in what eventually became a 38-point blowout win for his team.

At the end of the regular season, John Stockton had a respectable season as a backup rookie point guard. He averaged 5.6 points, 5.1 assists, and 1.3 steals while shooting 47% from the perimeter. Had John Stockton been a starter that played 36 minutes a night that season, he would have averaged a double-double of 11.1 points and ten assists. And with the way he played a starter in the few games he started for the Utah Jazz, it was easy to believe that John Stockton did indeed have the makings of a future double-double star playmaker.

As early as his rookie season, John Stockton would already feel what it was like to play for a team that had a chance for an NBA title when he helped the Jazz win 41 games to make the playoffs. In his four-year stay with Gonzaga, he never even got to the NCAA Tournament because of how mediocre the Bulldogs played. But with the Jazz in only his first season, he was playing with tested veterans like Green, Dantley, and Griffith. He did not have to carry the Jazz on his shoulders but would instead learn from his veteran teammates and the experience he gained after playing in a tough NBA postseason tournament.

John Stockton would make his playoff debut in Game 1 of the Utah Jazz's first-round series against the Houston Rockets led by Hakeem Olajuwon and Ralph Sampson, two seven-footers roaming and protecting the paint. In only 13 minutes of play in Game 1, Stockton had eight points, five rebounds, and six assists to help the Jazz steal one in Houston. However, he was not able to help his team in what would become a blowout loss to the Rockets in Game 2.

In Game 3, John Stockton was instrumental in giving the Utah Jazz a 2-1 advantage over the Houston Rockets. After playing only 14 minutes, Stockton would go for 11 points off the bench. Each of those 11 points mattered as the Jazz would win the game by only eight points. However, Stockton failed to score a single point when Houston defeated the Jazz by only two points in Game 4.

In what was a do-or-die Game 5 for John Stockton and his teammates, the Jazz would play an inspired brand of basketball against one of the title favorites that season. While Stockton only had five points and four assists, he was able to help out on the defensive end to frustrate the Rockets' guards. The frontcourt was doing all the damage for Houston while Utah's backcourt players defended their guards well to seal the win and the series for the Jazz.

Unfortunately for the Utah Jazz, they would run up against the Denver Nuggets, a high-scoring team led by dynamic players such as Fat Lever and Alex English. Matching up with the bigger and more athletic Lever was difficult for Stockton. Though he was not entirely a great scorer, Lever was an adept point guard at doing everything else. He rebounded, defended, and made plays for others. Game 1 was an indication as neither Stockton nor Green stood a chance against Lever, who finished with an amazing triple-double performance in a win for the Nuggets. Game 2 was more or less the same as Stockton had an off night while the opposing guards were negating Green's double-double night with their great performances. Utah would end up in a desperate 0-2 hole.

The Utah Jazz would edge out a win on their home floor in Game 3 to prevent a sweep from materializing. In that game, John Stockton finally broke out of his slump and finished with a new playoff high of 13 points on 5 out of eight from the field. And in Game 4, he did just as well by going his first playoff double-double. He finished that night with 12 points, ten assists, and four steals. However, the Jazz dropped to a 1-3 deficit with that loss. They were unable to save the series when they lost by 12 points in Game 5.

Despite bowing out of the playoffs in the second round, John Stockton's experience as a backup playmaker and rookie that played a lot of minutes in the playoffs would ultimately help him become a star in the future. While Stockton believed he could one day become a star, he was not alone in that belief. The man he backed up all season long, Ricky Green, had the same thought in his mind. After a practice that season, he once approached Frank Layden out of the blue to tell him that the rookie John Stockton had what it took to become a star when he saw what he was capable of in that session. Layden said that Green was the first player on the team to see the star potential in Stockton.[vii] However, the rise of that star would ultimately have to wait.

The Arrival of Karl Malone

If the Utah Jazz had just one problem the previous season, it was frontcourt scoring. The backcourt had no problem in that regard. Adrian Dantley, their starting small forward, was doing most of his damage as a midrange shooter. At that time, Darrell Griffith was the best three-point shooter in league history and was also a high-flying act that complemented the team's running style. Of course, both Rickey Green and John Stockton were effective at setting the tempo with their quickness and passing skills.

However, when they were forced to play the half court, the Utah Jazz had trouble getting points from their frontcourt. Mark Eaton was just a rebounder and shot-blocking presence. Meanwhile, Thurl Bailey did not have the strength or skill level to keep up with bigger frontcourts. They needed someone with size and skill at the frontcourt to balance out their scoring.

During June 1985, they had an opportunity to become a better team and give John Stockton the man that would finish his sweet passes. The 1985 Draft Class was headlined by Georgetown center Patrick Ewing, who could score down in the low post and defend the paint like an umbrella. Other future stars in that class included Chris Mullin and Joe Dumars. But arguably the best player of that class was the 6'9" bruising big man that played for Louisiana Tech.

Nicknamed "The Mailman" back in college because he would always deliver what was asked of him, Karl Malone was already a big bruiser back in college. The 6'9" power forward used his 250-pound frame to his advantage against smaller frontlines. He was a supreme inside scoring force and a terrific rebounder for Louisiana Tech back in college. But because the Utah Jazz had the 13th pick that season, Layden did not believe they could take him no matter how much they wanted him.[viii]

With the abilities that Karl Malone showed back in college, a lot of people thought he would have been taken within the top five along with big forwards such as Charles Oakley, Ed Pinckney, and Keith Lee. However, as 1985 draft unfolded, players were getting taken while Karl Malone's name was never called. All of the other top forwards had already been selected, and Malone was the sole top player at his position left.

Because Karl Malone was still available when the Utah Jazz had the opportunity to take a player that could change the fortune of the franchise, they would take The Mailman without any question. This time, however, the Utah Jazz fans erupted when they found out that Malone was coming to Salt Lake City. The Jazz would finally have the big man they needed to complement their backcourt's speed and playmaking skills. And for John Stockton, he had found the man that would be the second name of the soon-to-be-famous phrase "Stockton to Malone."

With Karl Malone in the fold, the Utah Jazz would have a complementary frontcourt piece that either Green or Stockton could pass to. They would nevertheless suffer through a minor setback when they lost Darrell Griffith to a leg injury before the season even started. Griffith would sit out the entire season and left the scoring duties to Adrian Dantley and Karl Malone. But The Mailman delivered, especially when it was Stockton who was dishing him dimes.

When the Jazz's regular season started on October 25, 1985, both John Stockton and Karl Malone sat on the bench to watch their more established teammates start the game in their place. Nevertheless, Stockton had a good night off the bench when he spelled the backcourt for 25 minutes. He had 11 points and 12 assists to kick off his second season with a double-double. Meanwhile, Malone only had eight points.

However, on October 30, the Jazz's third game, both Stockton and Malone would start for the first time together. The point guard finished the game with six points and nine assists while The Mailman delivered 13 points in 23 minutes. The duo was instrumental in giving Utah their first win of the regular season.

John Stockton would continue to start games in place of Rickey Green, who was momentarily relegated to the bench that season. In his second start of the season on November 1, he would go for his second double-double of 11 points and 14 assists in a win over the Phoenix Suns. The rookie Karl Malone also did not disappoint as a starter that could finish Stockton's passes.

On November 22, John Stockton would have his best game at that point in his career. In a win over the Cleveland Cavaliers, the sophomore NBA point guard out of Gonzaga would tie his career-high in points by going for 19 markers. He also finished the game with ten assists and five steals. A week later, he would have a similar performance by going for 17 points, ten assists, and a new career-best six steals in a loss to the Denver Nuggets.

John Stockton would once again outdo all of his previous performances on December 2, when the Utah Jazz met the

Golden State Warriors. The point guard would play 41 minutes and sink half of his 12 shots to score 14 points. More importantly, he finished that game with a new career-high of 17 assists. Stockton almost orchestrated that win by himself with Adrian Dantley, their best scorer, missing that game. His passes allowed seven other Jazz players to score at least nine points in that game.

In the next game, which was a meeting between the Utah Jazz and the Los Angeles Lakers, John Stockton would go toe-to-toe with Magic Johnson, who was known as the league's top point guard and best passer at that time. With Dantley back in the fold to score 36 points and with Malone scoring a new career high of 25 points, John Stockton finished the game with 17 assists just two nights after he also had the same number of dimes. Some would say that Dantley and Malone made it easy for him to collect those assists that night. However, the closer reality was that Stockton was making it easier for them to score by finding them in their best spots.

On December 20, John Stockton would once again tie his career-high in both assists and steals. In that loss to the Philadelphia 76ers, the 23-year-old point guard would go for eight points, 17 assists, and six steals. Judging by his stats, there was no arguing that Stockton was a gifted playmaker when given the possessions and minutes. However, the Jazz were not doing very well with him at the starting spot. He would lose the starting job to Rickey Green permanently on January 17, 1986. In the 39-game span in which he started or at least played starter's minutes, he was averaging 9.1 points, 8.5 assists, and 2.2 steals.

Though he was playing off the bench, John Stockton still delivered fine performances as a backup point guard. On January 29, he would go for 11 points and 12 assists in the Jazz's 21-point win over the Sixers. He then had at least five assists over the next nine games and was the sparkplug that made things easier for the Utah Jazz's backup players.

John Stockton would have two more double-doubles to end the season. He would go for ten points, 13 assists, and three steals on March 17 to give the Utah Jazz a win over the Detroit Pistons and Isaiah Thomas. Then on March 29, he would go for 13 points, 14 assists, and five steals in 31 minutes of play against the San Antonio Spurs in a win for the Jazz.

By the end of the regular season, John Stockton's numbers improved well enough. Once again playing 82 games, which included 38 starts, he averaged 7.7 points, 7.4 assists, and 1.9 steals. All of his numbers, including his efficiency from the field, improved in his second year. And though he was merely a backup point guard, he eclipsed Rickey Green as the team's top passer by leading the Utah Jazz in assists. He was also their best ball thief. Meanwhile, Karl Malone had a respectable rookie season after averaging 14.9 points and 8.9 rebounds. The two young future stars would lead the Jazz to a 42-win season to make the playoffs for only the third time in franchise history.

While Stockton may have performed well in the playoffs the last season, the 1986 playoffs were horrible to him. The Utah Jazz struggled against an upstart and high-scoring Dallas Mavericks. The Jazz would lose to the Mavs in four games as John Stockton would average only 6.8 points and 3.5 assists. Unlike the previous season, Stockton and the Utah Jazz would bow out of the playoffs early in the first round.

The Beginning of the Stockton and Malone Era

As the 1985-86 season ended and before the 1986-87 regular campaign got started, the Utah Jazz jumpstarted the dawn of a new era by trading away the man that was their best player since 1979 and the All-Star that led the franchise to their very first playoff appearance in 1984. The Jazz would decide to let go of Adrian Dantley in exchange for the Detroit Pistons' Kelly Tripucka.

Adrian Dantley was a significant loss for the Jazz because of his ability to put points on the board. During his time in Utah, he led the NBA in scoring twice and was able to average at least 30 points per game four straight years. And during the 1985-86 season, he finished a close second to Dominique Wilkins for the honor of being the league's top scorer. He was a talented shooter from the perimeter and was also great at running the floor for quick scoring opportunities.

As good of a player as Dantley was, he did not see eye to eye with Frank Layden. Since the 1984-85 season, the two had been feuding with one another.[ix] They were always seen arguing on the floor until the boiling point came. The relationship was broken and irreparable. Layden had to trade him away not because he wanted his younger core players to grow but because he was not helping the Jazz with his feud with the head coach. Dantley's move to Detroit would, however, help usher in the new era of Karl Malone as the team's best player. Of course, John Stockton was there to make things easy for him, though he reprised his role as the veteran Rickey Green's backup.

Though John Stockton was still the backup point guard, he was getting consistent minutes as one of the Jazz's most crucial players. Early on in the season on November 5, he would go for an excellent performance off the bench in a win over the

Cleveland Cavaliers. He had five points but finished with eight assists and six steals. One day later, he scored a new season high of 17 points on 7 out of 11 shooting from the field in a loss to the Denver Nuggets.

After struggling in the early portions of the season, John Stockton would go for his first double-double performance on December 5. He finished that win over the New York Knicks with 13 points, 14 assists, and four steals. A night later in a win in Sacramento, he finished with 11 points and 11 assists. Then, on December 10, he would go for 13 assists when the Jazz defeated the Denver Nuggets. Rounding out that four-game stretch of consecutive double-digit assists games, Stockton would go for 12 points and 13 dimes in a win over the Dallas Mavericks on December 11. During that four-game run, he averaged 11 points and 12.8 assists in only 26 minutes of play.

On January 8, 1987, the Utah Jazz faced a championship-caliber Los Angeles Lakers team in a battle between the present best point guard in the NBA and the playmaker that would soon become the best at his position. With John Stockton starting at the helm going up against Magic Johnson, the younger point guard took the game personally.

It was as if Stockton was a master puppeteer that controlled the entire tempo and outcome of the game. He was dropping dime after dime to make it easier for his teammates to score. Layden allowed the ball to go through Stockton's hands on every possession because every pass he made found an open teammate. At the end of that win over a powerhouse team, John Stockton had a new career high of 22 assists to go along with 11 points. While some players would have 20-10 games on points and assists or rebounds, Stockton did it by passing to his heart's content. That game was an indication of what John Stockton would be in the future—a superstar playmaker.

Three days after that career performance from John Stockton, the Utah Jazz would go to Seattle to play in front of some of the people that watched the Gonzaga product play ball since he was in grade school. Stockton did not disappoint by scoring over 20 points for the first time in his career. He made five of his ten field goal attempts and all 11 of his free throws to score a new career high of 21 points. However, Utah ended up losing that game to the Sonics.

Continuing what was still a marquee season for an in improving John Stockton, the young 24-year-old Gonzaga product would help his team defeat a powerhouse Boston Celtics squad on February 16 with his passing abilities. He only had nine points but finished the game with 17 assists and four steals to secure the win for the Utah Jazz. And eight days later, he would then help blow the Seattle SuperSonics out by 30 points when he finished the game with 17 points and 13 assists off the bench.

After that game against the Sonics, John Stockton would only have three more double-double performances to end the season but managed to make at least ten assists in seven of the Utah Jazz's final 28 games. In his last game of the regular season, he had 11 points and 11 assists in a loss to the Portland Trailblazers on April 17.

At the end of the regular 82-game campaign, John Stockton averaged improved numbers once again. He normed 7.9 points, 8.2 assists, and 2.2 steals despite playing fewer minutes than he did the year before. His field goal shooting also improved and had he played 36 minutes a night, he would have averaged 12.6 points, 13 assists, and 3.4 steals. Those numbers were reflective of what John Stockton was capable of if he was playing with a starter's minutes. And because he had improved so much alongside Karl Malone, who had risen to become a capable scorer and the Jazz's best player, Utah made the playoffs for a third consecutive season since drafting Stockton. They won 44 games during the regular season.

In the playoffs, the Utah Jazz met the Golden State Warriors in the first round. And for the first time in franchise history, they had home court advantage in the playoffs. At first, the advantage favored them when they won the first two games at home. Stockton did not even perform very well in those two games after averaging just four points and four assists. Nevertheless, they started the series with a 2-0 advantage.

As good as the Jazz had played in the first two games, they would suddenly plummet in the next three games. Stockton played marginally better in Game 3 after going for 13 points and eight rebounds in the Bay Area. However, the Warriors took that one from them. And in Game 4, he started in the playoffs for the first time that season and played 45 minutes. He would also finish with 15 points, 11 assists, and six steals. However, the Warriors used their superior firepower to beat the Jazz and to force Game 5. In Game 5, Stockton was again playing at a high level after going for 14 points, 13 assists, and three steals. But they would find themselves at the short end of the rope after losing three consecutive games in that series. For a second straight season, the Jazz would bow out of the postseason in the first round.

While the Utah Jazz once again failed to go deep into the playoffs, there were a lot of reasons for them to be hopeful for the future. For the second straight year, they improved their win-loss record despite the fact that they lost Adrian Dantley to a trade and that Darrell Griffith was still trying to get back to his stellar form. The reason for the improvement could be attested largely to how Stockton and Malone improved together as a duo.

John Stockton showed all season long what he could do if he was given more substantial minutes at the point guard spot. He was dropping dimes with ease and was making life easier for Karl Malone and the rest of the scorers. In many ways, he could see plays and make passes that Rickey Green could only dream of. It was his unselfish mentality and defensive skills at the point guard position that helped make the Jazz the best defensive team in the league.

For Malone's part, he was living up to the standard of what Layden had hoped he would become when he drafted him in 1985. Karl Malone became obsessed with fitness. He was always in the weight room trying to make himself stronger, faster, and more physically imposing than any other power forward in the NBA. With his strength, he could outmuscle his defender. And with his superior athletic gifts and speed, he could outrun any other big man in the league. Karl Malone had become a 20-10 double-double machine for the Utah Jazz, who were looking for a new go-to guy after trading away Dantley. They found one in Malone.

Since both John Stockton and Karl Malone were still young and improving, the Utah Jazz were only going to get scarier and better. With what the inside-outside duo had shown during the 1986-87 season, there was no arguing that Stockton and Malone would soon become the most dangerous guard-big man one-two punch in the entire NBA. And if they could keep that up, they had the makings of an all-time great basketball duo.

The Dime-Dropping Machine, Stockton's Rise to Stardom

With Rickey Green aging deeper into his 30's, Frank Layden began to understand that the better choice for the starting point guard position was his 25-year-old Gonzaga product. At that point in John Stockton's career, he had spent the last three seasons as a backup point guard that never got to play more than 24 minutes a night. But with the way he played in the few games that he started and when he was given starter's minutes, Stockton had proven that he could produce on both ends of the floor at a high level. It was finally time for him to take over as the team's best point guard.

It would take until the fourth game of the season for Layden to realize that he needed to put John Stockton in the starting position. Before taking over the starting spot on a permanent basis, he was averaging 12.3 points and six assists off the bench. However, he would begin to become a double-double machine when he was given the starting spot. On November 11, 1987, he earned his position. In that 29-point win over the Dallas Mavericks, he finished with 12 points and 14 assists.

As a starter, John Stockton orchestrated the offense to perfection and made it a point to make things easier for his teammates to score instead of trying to score the ball himself. During a six-game stretch from November 27 to December 8, he would have consecutive double-digit assists and averaged 13.8 points and 13.5 assists.

On December 14, John Stockton would have one of his best performances as a professional player when he had a terrific game against the Seattle Sonics. In that blowout win, he made nine of his ten field goal attempts to score a new career high of 26 points in addition to dishing out 16 assists and stealing six possessions. But John Stockton was just starting to scratch the surface.

Though it came at a losing effort, John Stockton would have a similar performance on January 2, 1988, for his second 20-10 game that season. He would finish that two-point loss to the Sacramento Kings with 21 points and a new season-high of 19 assists for a Utah Jazz team that seemed to have performed better with him leading the charge.

On January 30, John Stockton started to show that he had indeed developed into arguably the league's best pure point guard. He would have 17 consecutive double-double performances during that stretch. It started when he had 17 points and 19 assists in a win over the Atlanta Hawks. But it was the two back-to-back performances against the LA Clippers that made heads turn.

On February 19, in that first game of that back-to-back, Stockton would have 19 points, 21 assists, and eight steals for his third 20-10 game of the season. A night later, he replicated that feat by going for 21 assists yet again in addition to the 16 points and six steals he had in that game. Those were both wins for the Utah Jazz as their starting point guard seemingly toyed with the Clipper defense and had his teammates on a string like a master puppeteer.

John Stockton's 17-game double-double streak would end on March 7 when he failed to reach double-digit assists by only one dime. During those 17 games, Stockton was terrific after averaging 16.2 points, 15.6 assists, and 3.4 steals. He even had a field goal shooting clip of 60%, which is an incredible number for a point guard that played mostly on the perimeter. However, during that span of games, John Stockton failed to make the All-Star Team over equally deserving guards such as Magic Johnson, Fat Lever, Clyde Drexler, and Alvin Robertson. He was one of the biggest All-Star snubs that season.

Though he missed the All-Star Game, John Stockton continued to impress. On March 14, against the Denver Nuggets, he would have his first 20-20 game of his career after going for 24 points and 20 assists in that win. He achieved those numbers even though Karl Malone only played three minutes that night. That meant that Stockton did not always need Malone to pile up assists. It could even be argued that Malone needed him more to get good looks.

John Stockton was not done piling up career performances. In a loss to the Portland Trailblazers on April 14, he would go for 17 points and a new career-high 26 assists. At that time, those 26 assists were the fourth-highest single-game tally in league history. Then, in the final game of the regular season for the

Utah Jazz, Stockton helped defeat the Houston Rockets by going for a new career high in points of 27 in addition to tallying 18 assists.

At the end of the regular season, John Stockton averaged new career highs across the board. All of his numbers improved. He was averaging 14.7 points, a league-leading 13.8 assists, and three steals in 82 games. Stockton's 13.8 assists, at that time, placed him behind only Isiah Thomas' 13.9 assists during the 1984-85 season concerning most assists per game in a single season. He even shot an impressive 57.4% shooting clip and 84% accuracy from the free throw line. With how John Stockton was performing that season, he was rapidly becoming the best pure point guard in the league and was the only player that challenged Magic Johnson as the best player at that position. He was even named to the All-NBA Second Team that season.

The 47-win Utah Jazz would once again make the playoffs and had not missed the postseason since drafting John Stockton. The Jazz would meet the Portland Trailblazers in the first round. The Blazers were championship contenders with stars such as Clyde Drexler, Jerome Kersey, and Terry Porter leading the way. They were the favorites in that series.

The series started with a loss for the Utah Jazz in Portland. Stockton had 20 points and nine assists in that losing effort but would nevertheless perform better in Game 2. Aggressively attacking the basket to draw fouls, John Stockton finished the game with 20 points after making 16 of his 19 free throws. He also had 13 assists to give the Utah Jazz a steal in Game 2.

When the Utah Jazz headed home for Games 3 and 4, they would complete the series upset. Stockton had one of his better playoff performances in Game 3 when he went for 17 points, 16 assists, and four steals. Then, in Game 4, he had a new career playoff-high of 23 points to go along with ten assists and nine rebounds for a near triple-double. The Jazz would win Games 3 and 4 to head to the second round for the first time in the Stockton and Malone era.

The Utah Jazz would have their hands full in the second round as they were on their way to face the league-leading and defending champions the Los Angeles Lakers. And for John Stockton's part, he was going to match up with the bigger and more battle-tested Magic Johnson, who was regarded as the 80's best point guard. It was a battle between the man that would soon become the best playmaker and the established superstar at that position.

In Game 1, Stockton struggled against the bigger Johnson's defense and was limited to seven points on a three out of 13 shooting clip from the floor in that loss for the Jazz. But in Game 2, John Stockton was able to make up for it by going for 19 points and 13 assists to steal a win in Los Angeles. And when John Stockton had 22 points, 12 assists, and five steals in Game 3 to give the Utah Jazz a 2-1 lead, everyone thought that an upset was in the making.

But the Lakers proved why they were the defending champions. The Jazz could not muster up enough grit to prevent their opponents from scoring on their top-ranked defense in Game 4 as the Lakers tied the series. And in Game 5, Los Angeles took back the series lead despite the fact that John Stockton had one of the best performances a point guard could have in the playoffs. The Utah Jazz playmaker finished Game 5 with 23 points and 24 assists for his first playoff 20-20 game. And after tallying those 24 assists, Stockton also tied Magic Johnson for the single-game record for assists in the playoffs. That record still stands to this day.

The Utah Jazz proved that they were a team that would soon become a threat in the future when they finished Game 6 with a blowout win over the Lakers. Stockton had 14 points and 17 assists to help his team force Game 7. And in Game 7, Stockton once again had a fantastic performance after going for 29 points and 20 assists. However, the Lakers were simply too much, and the Jazz fell in seven games to the eventual champions.

Averaging 19.5 points, 14.8 assists, and 3.4 steals during the playoffs, John Stockton was even better in the postseason to prove that his team had the makings of a championship contender. And in that playoff battle against the Lakers, he even outplayed Magic Johnson, who averaged 18 points and 9.3 assists, by going for 19.3 points, 16.4 assists, and four steals. John Stockton was quickly becoming the best pure point guard in the NBA.

The 1988-89 season would be the proof that John Stockton was not a mere passing fancy and that he was already one of the best players at his position. His stellar 1987-88 season was not a fluke as Stockton would continue to rise up the ranks of the NBA's most elite players. It was during the upcoming season that he would prove himself as the heir-apparent for the mantle as the league's best point guard.

John Stockton would begin the 1988-89 season like a fumbling banker dropping dimes with ease. In his first 20 games of the season, he would have 17 games of dishing out double-digit assists. He even had two games of dishing out at least 20 dimes.

The first was when the Utah Jazz defeated the Phoenix Suns on November 19, 1988. He had 19 points, 21 assists, and seven steals that night. And then on December 7, Stockton had 18 points, 20 assists, and five steals in a win over the Washington Bullets. During that span of games, the Jazz were 13-7.

On January 3, 1989, John Stockton would have another 20-assist game and his first 20-20 performance of the season. In that loss to the Houston Rockets, he made 12 of his 16 shots from the field to score 26 points in addition to compiling 24 assists and stealing six possessions. And at the end of the month, Stockton would go for a new career high in points by going for 30 points for the first time in his career. In that win over Dallas, he had 30 points and 13 assists.

With John Stockton playing like he was the best point guard in the league, he was named to the All-Star team for the very first time alongside teammates Karl Malone and Mark Eaton. And because Magic Johnson was unable to play in the midseason classic, Stockton was selected to start for the Western All-Stars in place of the veteran point guard. He had 11 points and 17 assists to lead the way for the West to win. Teammate Karl Malone was named the MVP of that game.

On Valentine's Day, which was the first game after the All-Star Game, John Stockton would have another 20-20 game to prove that he was not only great at looking for the open man but had also improved so much to be a consistent scorer that could put up 20 points at any given night. In that win over the Denver Nuggets, Stockton had 22 points, 21 assists, and three steals in an efficient six out of eight shooting night for him.

From February 27 to April 22, which was the end of the regular season, John Stockton outdid himself by going for 27 straight games of double-doubles on points and assists. He started when he had 25 points and 15 assists in a win over the New Jersey Nets. And in arguably his best individual performance during that stretch, he had 19 points, 20 assists, and eight steals in a narrow loss to the Mavericks on April 21 just one night before the regular season ended.

In John Stockton's first All-Star season, he once again improved from the previous season. He averaged new career highs in points and steals after going for 17.1 and 3.2 respectively. He also added 13.6 assists and would once again lead the league in that category for the second consecutive season. Those numbers were, at that time, third all-time in most assists per game in a single season by a player. Stockton, who led the Utah Jazz to their first 50-win game at 51 wins, was named to the All-NBA Second Team.

But as good as John Stockton, Karl Malone, and the rest of the Utah Jazz played that season, their top-ranked defense had no chance against a high-scoring team effort by the Golden State Warriors in the playoffs. The Jazz, who had home court advantage in the first round, got swept out of the postseason in just three games played. Stockton averaged 27.3 points, 13.7 assists, and 3.7 steals in that series.

Though the Utah Jazz fell early in the first round, one bright spot for the team that season was how John Stockton and Karl Malone improved as a duo. One reason for that was because Frank Layden, who had retired from coaching in the middle of the season to move to the front office, had given control over the team to Jerry Sloan. Sloan, who was an assistant for Layden, was known for his pick-and-roll offense. And when he was finally made the head coach, the pick-and-roll became more effective especially considering that he focused it so much on Stockton and Malone.

The two All-Stars complemented each other so well under Jerry Sloan. Stockton was a supreme unselfish passer that saw passes no other point guard could make. Meanwhile, when on the run, a physically imposing and athletic Karl Malone was unstoppable after catching the ball from Stockton. It was because of the pick-and-roll that the duo improved. Stockton could score off of it whenever defenses would focus on Malone after the screen. Meanwhile, Malone also improved as a scorer because of how many opportunities he was getting from that pick-and-roll set. It was under Jerry Sloan that Stockton and Malone and the phrase "Stockton to Malone" would become legendary.

Historic Assists Seasons

It was during the 1989 season when John Stockton began to rise as the best point guard in the entire league, not because of his scoring, but because he had grown so much as a supreme passer especially in the pick-and-roll. It was because of his unselfish nature and ability to play the pick-and-roll to perfection that helped John Stockton put up historic numbers in what can arguably be considered the best two-year stretch of his career.

Stockton opened the season on November 3, 1989, with 23 points and 19 assists in a win over the Denver Nuggets. He then finished the next seven games posting at least 15 assists in all of those outings. At one stretch, he even had 18 assists for three straight games during that personal run. He would average 20 points, 17 assists, and 4.4 steals in his first eight games.

On December 19, John Stockton would outdo himself and make history once more. In that loss to the New York Knicks, Stockton would post 18 points and a new career high of 27 assists. Those 27 assists, at that time, ranked as the third-highest assists total a player had in a single game. He tied Geoff Huston, who did it in 1982, in that regard.

After that game, John Stockton continued to dish out assists at a high rate. He would have at least ten or more assists in 33 outings over his next 37 games of that season. During that span, he was averaging 14.4 assists. This included three 20-20 games in a span of games that saw him making a second consecutive All-Star Game start. The first 20-20 game was on February 22, 1990, when he had 24 points and 20 assists in a win over the LA Clippers. Then on March 1, he had 26 points and 21 assists in a win over the Blazers. Two days after that, he had 22 points and 20 assists in a victory over the San Antonio Spurs.

John Stockton would have back-to-back 20-assist games on March 13 and 15, but would outdo that as an attacker two days after. On March 17, in a loss to the Sacramento Kings, Stockton would go for 14 out of 22 from the field and six out of nine from the free throw line to score a new career high of 34 points. That was only the second time he scored 30 or more points. And after that 21-assist game on March 13, John Stockton would post double-digit assists until the end of the regular season. He had three more 20-assist games during that span.

At the end of the regular season, John Stockton averaged new career highs in points and assists. He was norming 17.2 points, 14.5 assists, and 2.7 steals in the 78 games he played. With the 14.5 assists he averaged that year, John Stockton finally eclipsed Isiah Thomas for the single-season record for assists per game. It was the first time a player has averaged at least 14 assists a night in a single season. Up to this date, no other player has surpassed 14 assists per game or even eclipsed John Stockton's single-season record for most assists per game. It is a record that has stood for nearly 30 years, and no player has come close to breaking it. He also set the record for most assists totals in a single season after tallying 1,134 that season.

After helping the Utah Jazz win a new franchise high of 55 games during that season to make the playoffs, John Stockton would match up against another All-NBA point guard in the Phoenix Suns' Kevin Johnson. Though the Jazz had home court advantage and with Stockton averaging 15 points and 15 assists the entire series, the Suns came away with the upset after beating Utah in five games. For a second consecutive season, the Jazz were unable to break past the first round despite having home court advantage.

John Stockton would have an equally historic year the following season. During the 1990-91 season, he would continue to put up high numbers as a point guard. After dishing out at least ten assists in 15 of his first 18 games, Stockton would go for his first 20-20 game of the season on December 8, 1990. He had 27 points, 23 assists, and four steals in that win over the Los Angeles Clippers.

After going for at least 11 assists in the next 16 games, in which he averaged 14.2 points and 14.3 assists, Stockton would eclipse his previous best performances in a win over the San Antonio Spurs on January 15, 1991. In his second 20-20 game of the regular season, John Stockton would go for 20 points, 28 assists, and eight steals. Those 28 assists became Stockton's career best.

Aside from the fact that his 28-assist performance was his all-time career best, it was also the third all-time in most assists a player had in a single game. He tied Bob Cousy and Guy Rodgers in that regard. Only Scott Skiles, who recorded an all-time high of 30 assists earlier in the season, and Kevin Porter are ahead of him. Stockton's 27-assist and 26-assist games would later move to fourth and fifth all-time respectively. Since the 1983-84 season, Stockton has owned the record for second, third, and fourth all-time in assists in a single game. Only Scott Skiles has had more assists in a single game than Stockton since 1983. After putting up double-digit assists all season long, John Stockton would make the All-Star Game for the third time but would not end up as a starter because of Kevin Johnson.

After the midseason classic, John Stockton would have 34 double-digit assist games over the final 35 bouts. He also had 33 double-doubles during that span. His best passing performance was on March 11. In that loss to the San Antonio Spurs, he had 12 points, 20 assists, and six steals. He would only have one 20-assist performance during those final 35 games for the Utah Jazz.

For the sixth time in his seven-year career, John Stockton played all 82 games of the season to showcase his freakish durability and stamina. During that season, he averaged 17.2 points, 14.2 assists, and 2.9 steals. Those 14.2 assists rank second in all-time assists per game in a single season. And after totaling 1,164 assists during the 1990-91 season, John Stockton became the all-time leader in most assists dished out in a single season. No player has come close to breaking that record since then. After that campaign, John Stockton owned the top three records in most assists in a single season.

After making the playoffs for a seventh straight season since he was drafted in 1984, John Stockton would lead the 54-win Utah Jazz in the first-round matchup against Kevin Johnson and the Phoenix Suns. Losing only one game in that four-game series, the Utah Jazz would finally break into the second round as Stockton averaged 18 points and 12.8 assists in that matchup.

The Utah Jazz would face a 63-win and championship-favorite Portland Trailblazers in the second round of the playoffs. With the odds against them in Game 1, the Jazz would lose by 20 points despite Stockton's 18 points and 15 assists. They would then fall in Game 2 though the star point guard finished with 23 points and 16 assists.

After escaping a sweep after going down 0-2, the Utah Jazz would win Game 3 at home as John Stockton finished with 18 points and 15 assists. However, that was the best fight that the Utah Jazz were able to muster up. The Portland Trailblazers would manage to fend off the resilient Jazz team in the next two games, which were all close finishes, to make it to the Western Conference Finals.

After putting up two consecutive historic seasons, John Stockton had already secured his spot as the best pure point guard in the NBA and had even planted his name in the annals of basketball history as one of its best passers. However, John Stockton was yet to win a championship or even come close to competing for that trophy. That was the only knock to his legacy at that juncture of his career. If Stockton wanted to secure his place as an all-time great, the only way to do it was to win a title or at least reach the NBA Finals.

Falling Short

While John Stockton had made a name for himself as the NBA's best point guard especially after Magic Johnson retired from basketball, the problem he had was that his Utah Jazz were always struggling against tough competition in the playoffs. That was the theme during Stockton's career at that point in his life. And it would not be much different for him during the early part of the 90's, which was considered one of the most competitive eras of the NBA.

Reprising his role as the NBA's best passer, John Stockton would have double-digit assists in all but one of the first 20 games he played during the 1991-92 season. And on November 29, 1991, he even had his first 20-20 game of the season after going for 21 points and 23 assists in a blowout win over the Golden State Warriors early in the season.

From December 11 to January 22, 1992, John Stockton would pile up a 20-game streak of consecutive double-digit assist games. He had 19 double-doubles during that span. One of his better performances at that juncture was when he had a season-high of 27 points and 17 assists in a win over the LA Clippers on December 26. He would go on to average 16.4 points and 15.1 assists during that 20-game run.

Proving himself as one of the NBA's best defenders at the point guard position, John Stockton even had a 25-game streak in which he had at least one steal from January 10 to March 3. He averaged 3.1 steals during that span of games. His best defensive performance during that streak was when he had a season high of seven assists in addition to the 24 points he scored and 19 assists he dished out on February 11 in a win over the Cleveland Cavaliers.

Wrapping up another tremendous All-Star season for himself, John Stockton would end his regular season with two of his three 20-assist games. On April 17, he had nine points, 23 assists, and five steals in a win over the Minnesota Timberwolves. Two days later in the Jazz's final game of the season, the Jazz would beat the San Antonio Spurs as Stockton finished with 17 points, 21 assists, and four steals.

For a second time in his career, John Stockton would lead the league in assists and steals in the same season. He averaged 15.8 points, 13.7 assists, and three steals. After collecting 1,126 assists that season, John Stockton had become the leader of the top four assists seasons in NBA history. No other player since then has come close to eclipsing John Stockton's fourth-best assist season. Stockton would also lead the Jazz to a 55-win that season to tie their franchise-best in wins.

John Stockton would have a field day in the Jazz's first two games in the first-round series against the Los Angeles Clippers. In Game 1, he had ten points and 21 assists. Then, in Game 2, Stockton finished the night with 21 points and 19 assists. The Utah Jazz would win both games by double digits to claim a 2-0 series lead over the Clippers. However, the Clippers would manage to win the next two games on their home floor. Not willing to lose in the first round again, the Jazz would win an all-or-nothing Game 5 to make it to the second round against the Seattle SuperSonics.

The second-round matchup against the Sonics was when John Stockton faced a young and upstart defensive-minded point guard Gary Payton in the playoffs. While Payton would later become the best point guard in the league, Stockton owned that distinction at that point in history. He led the Jazz past the Sonics in only five games after averaging 14.2 points, 14 assists, and 3.2 steals in that series.

With a chance to make it all the way to the NBA Finals for the first time in his career and franchise history, John Stockton and the Jazz would face the Portland Trailblazers in a rematch of the previous season's Western Conference Semi-Finals. But similar to the last year, the Blazers overpowered the Jazz in Games 1 and 2 to gain a 2-0 advantage over Utah.

The Utah Jazz would, however, go on to win Games 3 and 4 to tie the series up at 2-2. John Stockton averaged 16 points and 12.5 assists in those two wins at home for the Utah Jazz. However, John Stockton had two of his worst performances in the playoffs that season in Games 5 and 6. He shot only 24% from the field while averaging just 12 points and 11 assists in those two games. With Stockton performing at his worst during the playoffs, the Utah Jazz would fail to make it to the NBA Finals after losing to the Blazers in six games.

The Utah Jazz would see themselves falling off during the 1992-93 season, especially considering that the Utah Jazz roster was changing with John Stockton and Karl Malone being the only constants of that team. Nevertheless, the duo was still arguably the best inside-outside combination in the NBA, and the Stockton and Malone tandem was still in its prime.

After starting the first 19 games of the season with 15 double-digit assist outputs, John Stockton would go for a new season-high in dimes on December 18, 1992. In that win over the Philadelphia 76ers, Stockton finished arguably his best performance at that juncture with 17 points, 22 assists, and two steals in only 32 efficient minutes. Ten days later, Stockton would have his second 20-assist game of the season after going for 13 points, 20 dimes, and seven steals in a win over the Minnesota Timberwolves.

While John Stockton might have slowed down as a dime-dishing point guard especially since the Jazz were slowing down and missing some of their key scorers, he would still muster up a 13-game double-digit assist streak from January 9 to February 1, 1993. During that run, he averaged 15.3 points and 13 assists. His best output during that run was when he had 18 assists in a win over the LA Lakers on January 22.

On February 13, John Stockton would go on to have his first and only 30-point game of the season. In that loss to the Atlanta

Hawks, he would go for 12 out of 16 from the floor and 4 out of 7 from the three-point area to go for a new season high of 32 points in addition to the nine assists and five steals that he had. Shortly after that, Stockton would make it to the All-Star Game as a starter. Leading the West to an overtime victory over the East, he had nine points and 15 assists as he and Karl Malone ran the pick-and-roll to perfection. The Jazz duo would be named co-MVPs of the 1993 All-Star Game.

Stockton would end the final 31 games of the regular season with 24 double-digit assist games. His best assist output during that run was when he had 19 dimes in a loss to the Golden State Warriors on February 24. Then, on April 17, he finished a game against the Phoenix Suns with 11 points, 18 assists, and four steals to help the Utah Jazz earn a much-needed win to avoid a low playoff position.

For a sixth-straight season, John Stockton would lead the league in assists after averaging 12 dimes in addition to the 15.1 points and 2.4 assists that he also normed that season. He was named to the All-NBA Second Team after leading the Utah Jazz to the playoffs for the ninth time since he was drafted. However, the Utah Jazz only mustered up 47 wins after seeing a slight tumble in the team's defense.

Battling an improved Seattle SuperSonics team, John Stockton matched up with Gary Payton in the first round of the playoffs for a second straight season. However, Payton had improved considerably and frustrated John Stockton on the offensive end. After winning Games 2 and 3, the Jazz ended up falling in five games with Stockton averaging only 13.2 points and 11 assists in that series.

While the Utah Jazz may have improved a bit after adding veteran pieces like Tom Chambers and Jeff Hornacek during the 1993-94 season, they would still lack what it took to compete for a championship at a time when the league was wide open for a new championship after Michael Jordan, who had led the Chicago Bulls to three straight titles, decided to retire. However, it did not take anything away from another one of John Stockton's fantastic seasons as the NBA's most elite passing point guard.

In one of Stockton's best stretches during that season, he would go for 13 consecutive double-digit assist games from December 11, 1993, to January 7, 1994. During that stretch, he averaged 15 points and 14.2 assists. His best performance during that time was when he had 18 points, 16 assists, and four steals in a win over the Washington Bullets on December 18.

John Stockton would mount another 13-game double-digit assist streak later in the season. It started on January 13 when he had 11 points and 14 assists. His best output during that span of games was when he had a season-best 26 points together with 13 assists in a win over the Houston Rockets on February 1. He averaged 14.5 points and 14.2 assists in that streak, which spanned until February 5.

On February 23, John Stockton would go for a new season high in what was arguably the best performance by the 32-year-old point guard that season. In that double-overtime victory over the San Antonio Spurs, Stockton went for 31 points, 14 assists, and three steals. With more fantastic performances under his belt, he would then go for 18 points, a season-high 20 assists, and five steals in an efficient win over the Phoenix Suns on March 6.

After ending the regular season with a total of 58 double-doubles, John Stockton would average 15.1 points, 12.6 assists, and 2.4 steals to get named to the All-NBA First Team. For a seventh straight season, he would lead the league in assists per game. He also helped the Utah Jazz improve their record to 53-29 that season to qualify for the playoffs once again in a span of ten seasons.

The Utah Jazz would meet an improved San Antonio Spurs team in the first round. While battling the Spurs on their home floor for Game 1, Stockton had a horrible outing. In that blowout loss, he shot 1 out of 4 from the field to score just three points in addition to dishing out only eight assists. He would also have a mediocre outing in Game 2 after finishing with 17 points and five assists. However, the Jazz still stole that game away from the Spurs.

Playing in Utah for Games 3 and 4, the Jazz would seem like an inspired team that were tired of bowing out early in the playoffs. John Stockton would finish with 13 points and 12 assists in a 33-point win for the Jazz, who had taken a 2-1 lead. Finally taking care of the Spurs in four games, the Jazz would win Game 4 after seeing Stockton go for 13 points and 18 assists.

In the second round, the Utah Jazz would meet a Denver Nuggets team that was led by the upstart 7'2" defensive center Dikembe Mutombo. Not impressed by the 42-win Nuggets, Stockton and company would race ahead to a 3-0 lead over the lower-seeded team. In Game 3, Stockton had his best performance of the playoffs after going for 24 points and 13 assists.

But even after going for an insurmountable 3-0 lead, the Utah Jazz got a scare from the Denver Nuggets. Not willing to submit to their circumstance, the Nuggets went on to win Games 4 to 6 to tie the series and to force Game 7. However, the Nuggets were unable to make history after the Jazz defeated them in a do-or-die final game. The Utah Jazz would secure a date with the Houston Rockets for a chance to make the NBA Finals for the first time in franchise history.

While the Jazz seemingly had a chance to make the Finals, they merely became one of the victims to a rampaging Hakeem Olajuwon, who was playing the best brand of basketball any center could on every play. The league MVP would toy with the Jazz defense to average 28 points on Utah's hapless frontline. In the end, Stockton would once again fall short of making the Finals after his Jazz fell to the Rockets in five games.

Sporting the same supporting cast but surrounding John Stockton and Karl Malone with several more veterans, the Utah Jazz were on their way to having the best record in franchise history during the 1994-95 season. But at age 32, John Stockton's window to win a championship was already closing. However, winning a title was never as difficult as it was at that time because of the rise of several conference powerhouses such as the Houston Rockets, the San Antonio Spurs, the Phoenix

Suns, and the Seattle SuperSonics. Despite the odds, the Stockton and Malone pick-and-roll duo was still deemed the most unstoppable two-man play in basketball.

With John Stockton still playing at a high level at age 32, he would have 13 double-doubles early in the first 20 games of the season. He went for three 20-10 outputs and had a season-high of 27 points together with ten assists on November 5, 1994, in a loss to the Seattle Sonics in just the second game of the regular season. And in his best performance at that early juncture, he went for 25 points and 12 assists in a win over the Phoenix Suns on November 21.

On January 7, 1995, John Stockton would have his first 20-assist game. In only 30 minutes of action in a blowout win over the Philadelphia 76ers, Stockton went for ten points and a new season-high of 20 assists. And nine days later, he would go for 15 points and 19 assists in a win over the Indiana Pacers. All of those assists contributed well to what Stockton would achieve later in the season.

On February 1 of that year, John Stockton would break a record and make history. In only 860 games (compared to Johnson's 874 games) in a career that spanned 11 seasons, John Stockton would make a bounce pass to Karl Malone, who converted the basket in the six-minute mark of the second quarter, to record 9,922 total assists. With that assist to Malone, Stockton became the new leader for most career assists and would never relinquish that leadership even to this day. With that accomplishment, he effectively became the best passer in league history. Stockton ended that 41-point win over the Denver Nuggets with 12 points and 16 assists.

After making another All-Star appearance, the best passer in league history would go on to have 16 double-doubles in the final 22 games of the regular season to once again lead the league in assists. As an eight-time leader in assists, John Stockton tied Bob Cousy, the man he was often compared to, in that regard. He would also tie Cousy's record for most consecutive seasons as the leader in assists.

At the end of the regular season, John Stockton would once again play 82 seasons to prove his reputation as one of the league's iron men even at age 33. He averaged 14.7 points, 12.3 assists, and 2.4 steals. And with him at the helm of an efficient offensive attack that also focused more on defense, the Utah Jazz won a new franchise record of 60 games to secure a spot as a top three team in the Western Conference.

While the Utah Jazz may have entered the 1995 playoffs with the home court advantage against the Houston Rockets in the first round, they would face an unstoppable force in the middle. Hakeem Olajuwon, who had won a title season before in a historic run, would become even more unstoppable during the 1995 playoffs. He singlehandedly destroyed the Utah Jazz to average 35 points, 8.6 rebounds, and four assists in five games. Nothing that the Jazz threw at him worked, and the Rockets would once again eliminate them in the first round despite the fact that Stockton and Malone had just led the team to a franchise record in wins.

John Stockton's chances of winning a title only became slimmer as Michael Jordan returned to the Chicago Bulls for the 1995-96 season to once again become the leader of a championship-favorite team. Nevertheless, consistency has always been one of the critical attributes of the Jazz since drafting Stockton back in 1984. And as long as John Stockton and Karl Malone were playing at a high level, the Utah Jazz would always have a chance to fight for the championship.

Even though he was already aging past his prime, John Stockton was still one of the premier point guards in the NBA and was still the league's best passer. He recorded 12 double-doubles early in their first 20 games. He had five 20-10 performances, which included one of his best outings that season. He had 29 points and 12 assists over the Toronto Raptors on November 13, 1995.

Though Father Time was already catching up with him, John Stockton was still able to pull off streaks of double-digit assist games because of how effective he and Malone ran the pick-and-roll under Jerry Sloan's direction. From January 27 to February 22, 1996, he had a 12-game streak of double-digit assists. He averaged 17.3 points and 11.7 assists during that run. His best scoring output during that time was when he had 16 dimes in a win in San Antonio on February 13. And in the game before that, right before he made his eighth All-Star appearance, he had 28 points and ten assists in a loss to the Dallas Mavericks.

John Stockton's season high in points was on March 5, when he had 30 points on nine out of 15 shooting from the field in a win over the Sacramento Kings. And after that, he would go on to record 16 double-digit assists in the Utah Jazz's final 25 games to once again make sure that he was the league's top passer in one of the best teams in the Western Conference.

At the end of another All-Star season for John Stockton, he would average 14.7 points, 11.2 assists, and 1.7 steals in 82 games. For the ninth consecutive season, he would lead the league in assists. And because of that accomplishment, John Stockton became the all-time leader in most seasons as the league's highest assists man. No player has yet to come close to breaking Stockton's nine seasons as the NBA's assists leader.

The league's nine-time assists leader would go on to have 11 points and 23 assists in Game 1 of the Utah Jazz's first-round matchup versus the Portland Trailblazers. He would then have 16 dimes in Game 2 to give the Jazz a 2-0 series lead. And although the Blazers managed to win Games 3 and 4, Stockton would go for 21 points and 11 assists in a 38-point win in Game 5 to give the Jazz a ticket to the second round.

John Stockton would then open their second-round matchup against the San Antonio Spurs with 13 points and 19 assists in a win for the Utah Jazz. And after easy wins in Games 3 and 4 to lead the series 3-1, Stockton and company would lose Game 5. However, in Game 6, the Jazz would play like an inspired team on both ends of the floor to win the game by 27 points. Stockton had 13 assists in that win to give the Jazz another Western Conference Finals appearance.

Standing in the way of John Stockton's chance to make it to the NBA Finals were the Seattle Sonics, headed by Gary Payton. At that time, Payton was making a name as arguably the best point guard in the league, not because he could run a team like Stockton, but because of his ability to put points up on the board and defend the perimeter at the highest level possible. He was the 1996 Defensive Player of the Year and only the fifth guard to do so in league history.

With Gary Payton putting the clamps on John Stockton in Game 1, the Sonics would come out with a 30-point win in Game 1 as the Utah Jazz point guard would finish with only four points and seven assists. It was the same story in Game 2. Stockton had only 11 points and seven assists as the Seattle Sonics went up 2-0 in the series because of the incredible defense that Payton was playing on the star point guard. Fortunately for the Jazz, they would not go down 3-0 when they won Game 3 by 20 points though Stockton would only have seven points and six assists in that game.

Failing to go for a double-double in what was another terrible game for him, John Stockton would have seven points and eight assists in Game 4 as the Sonics raced ahead to a 3-1 series lead to the dismay of the Utah Jazz. But even though they were in a hole, the Jazz never quit. They would win Game 5 on the road though John Stockton only had four points and six assists.

John Stockton would finally get himself loose in Game 6 to help the Utah Jazz force a deciding Game 7. In that 35-point win in Game 6, he had 14 points and 12 assists for his first and only double-double that series. He would once again do well when he had 22 points, eight rebounds, seven assists, and four steals in Game 7, but it was not enough to beat the Sonics in Seattle. In the end, the Jazz would fall short once again, and John Stockton would average just 9.9 points and 7.6 assists in that seven-game series.

The Back-to-Back Finals Appearances, Losing to the Bulls

After falling short of an NBA Final several times in the last few seasons, John Stockton and the Utah Jazz would finally get over the hump in the 1996-97 season. It was during that time when the Jazz and their all-time dynamic duo would become major stories not only in the league at that time but also in the history of the NBA.

Flanked by a fantastic supporting cast of veterans and capable role players such as Jeff Hornacek, Byron Russell, Antoine Carr, and Greg Ostertag, the duo of John Stockton and Malone would win 15 consecutive games early in the season to go 17-3 in their first 20 games of the season. John Stockton would average 13.7

points, 12.1 assists, and 2.1 steals during those 15 consecutive wins.

While the Utah Jazz struggled during late December and early January of 1997, the team ultimately steered right back on track and would finish the month of February with a 9-3 record. Stockton would see another All-Star appearance that month and would average 14.2 points, 11.6 assists, and 1.8 steals during February of 1997. His best performance that month was when he had 19 points and 13 assists in a win over the Toronto Raptors on February 27. Those were fantastic numbers for a man that was turning 35 later that year.

The Utah Jazz would get back on track by winning 15 consecutive games from March 12 to April 11. John Stockton started the streak by going for a season-high 31 points together with 11 assists and six rebounds against the New Jersey Nets. He then had 22 points and 15 assists in a win over the Denver Nuggets on March 23. During that run, he was averaging 14.5 points and 10.2 assists.

With the way John Stockton and Karl Malone led the Utah Jazz that season, they went for a new franchise record of 64 wins to eclipse the 60-win season they had two years ago. This time, however, they were not going to fall short and would mount what would become a defining run to the Finals. Karl Malone was named the season MVP while John Stockton averaged 14.4 points and 10.5 assists. Stockton would fail to lead the league in assists for the first time in ten seasons.

The conference-leading Utah Jazz would start their run to the Finals with a meeting with the Los Angeles Clippers in the first round of the playoffs. Stockton had 13 points and 17 assists in Game 1 to pave the way for the Jazz the entire season. He would then help his team complete the sweep by going for 12 points and 13 assists in Game 3 to easily proceed to the next round.

Still going up against an LA-based team, the Jazz would face the Lakers in the second round. Back then, the Lakers had Shaquille O'Neal, who was regarded as the most dominant player in the NBA, and a rookie named Kobe Bryant, another future Hall-of-Famer. While the Lakers may have had the talent, the Jazz had the superior team dynamics. They would take Games 1 and 2 before losing in Game 3. And after winning Game 4, the Jazz would proceed to the Conference Finals on the strength of Stockton's 24 points and ten assists. That win secured a matchup against the Houston Rockets, who had ousted the Jazz from the playoffs in 1994 and 1995. The 1997

Conference Finals would be the best time for them to take revenge.

While the Rockets may have had three all-time greats in Hakeem Olajuwon, Charles Barkley, and Clyde Drexler, there was no stopping the Jazz's pick-and-roll offense, team chemistry, and hunger. They would easily win Game 1 of the Conference Finals. John Stockton finished with 16 points and 13 assists to draw first blood. He would then have 26 points and 12 assists in Game 2 to give the Jazz a 2-0 series lead.

While the Houston Rockets may have won Games 3 and 4 to tie the series at two wins apiece, the Utah Jazz would come back strong in Game 5 to take back the lead and moved within one win away from making a trip to the NBA Finals for the first time in franchise history. It was also in Game 6 of that series when John Stockton made his mark.

With the game tied at 100, everything came down to the Utah Jazz's final possession. Either it was going to overtime, where the Rockets had a chance to force Game 7, or a win for the Jazz. John Stockton had something to say about that. With 2.8 seconds left on the game clock, Jerry Sloan called a play for John Stockton to get the ball 12 feet away from the top of the key and with Karl Malone screening two men from him. After getting the ball, Stockton dribbled once to get into position at the top of the key and found himself open for a three-point shot. As time was winding down, the shot hit the bottom of the net and the Jazz were heading to the NBA Finals for the first time in franchise history.

Often called "The Shot" among the Utah faithful and arguably the biggest shot in Utah Jazz franchise history, there was no doubt or fear in John Stockton when he took that game-winner. But even after draining what is still considered the biggest play in the history of the Utah Jazz, all John Stockton could do after that play was to give props to his teammates by saying that he could only hit that shot because everyone did exactly what they were supposed to do. While other teams and players often panicked in the final play of the game, Stockton saw that his team full of veterans did the right thing and followed the instructions to the letter. And when all of his teammates played their role the same way as they did all season long, he led them to victory with that historic shot.

History seemed to be on the side of the Utah Jazz after John Stockton made the biggest shot of his life, and things would eventually turn out to be tougher for his team because they were on their way to face the Chicago Bulls, who had won four of the last six NBA titles. That was the start of what was to become a two-year rivalry between arguably the two best teams of the 90's era.

Game 1 was a tight affair in Chicago. It all came down to the final plays of the game. John Stockton gave the Jazz the lead when he drained a three-pointer to answer the Bulls' Scottie Pippen's shot from beyond the arc. The Jazz were leading by one point with 52 seconds left, but Jordan would tie the game up with 36 seconds remaining after hitting half of his two free throws. But when Karl Malone had the opportunity to ice the game if he had hit all of his free throws, Pippen told him the phrase, "Just remember, the mailman doesn't deliver on Sundays, Karl." Indeed, The Mailman failed to deliver on that Sunday when he missed both free throws. Michael Jordan would then hit a jumper at the other end to give the Bulls a 1-0 lead.

After almost winning Game 1 on the road in Chicago, the Utah Jazz were out of it in Game 2. The Bulls dominated them from the opening tip and the Jazz would fall 0-2 in the franchise's first appearance in the NBA Finals. However, they were not out of the dance yet and would go on to perform at their best in Games 3 and 4.

Stockton and company were on their way to a blowout, but the Bulls tried to mount a comeback in Game 3. However, Utah stemmed the tide as Stockton finished the game with 17 points and 12 assists. John Stockton was the biggest name in Game 4. He shifted the momentum of the game after hitting a three-pointer to cut the Bulls' lead to two points late in the game.

After Jordan hit a jumper, Stockton stole the ball from him and got fouled over at the other end where he hit his free throws. And after a Bulls miss, it was John Stockton who grabbed the rebound and threw a full-court pass to a streaking Karl Malone, who made a layup that put the Jazz up by a single point. Stockton was seen jumping up and down after hitting Malone with that assist. The Jazz would never relinquish the lead as the series tied at two wins apiece.

Game 5 was the famous flu game that Michael Jordan played despite barely having the energy to run down the court. In hindsight, it was the Jazz's game to lose because they were unable to take advantage of a weakened and slow Jordan, who still managed to hit his long shots. It was MJ's three-pointer late in the game that gave the Chicago Bulls the lead for good with just 25 seconds left. That win gave the Bulls a 3-2 series lead heading into Game 6 in Chicago.

The Utah Jazz had a chance to force Game 7 by winning Game 6. It was another tight affair as both teams played terrific defense to force the game to go into another tight affair in the final seconds. The Bulls had possession of the ball in what was supposed to be the final play of the game. While the Jazz thought that the final shot would go through Jordan, the Greatest Player of All Time drew the double team near the left high post and made a pass to teammate Steve Kerr, who hit an open 17-footer to ice the game for the Bulls. That was the play of the game as Scottie Pippen disrupted the Utah Jazz's final opportunity to tie the game.

As the dust settled, the Chicago Bulls were named the NBA champions for the fifth time and a second consecutive year. Meanwhile, the Utah Jazz were left stunned and shocked by the turn of events. John Stockton, who averaged 15 points and 8.8 assists in the series, was unable to win what could have been the first title in his career. At 35 years old, that could have been his final shot at the NBA title, and it was back to the drawing board for him and the Utah Jazz.

It would turn out that the Utah Jazz were just as hungry heading into the 1997-1998 season as they were when they made that run to the Finals during the 1996-97 season. With the way they played the Bulls in the 1997 Finals, the Stockton and Malone-led Jazz proved that they could hang with the best. The only thing they needed to do during the 1997-98 season was to show they were the best by beating the best.

Unfortunately for John Stockton, he would not be available to help his team win at the early juncture of the season. Stockton, who had only missed four games at that point in his career, would have to miss time to recover from a surgery to remove loose cartilage in his left knee. One of the league's iron men, he was already feeling the effects of a long career full of battles and physical plays. The fact that he had only missed four games at that point in his career was already a testament to how tough of a player Stockton was even as he aged deeper into his 30's. That kind of toughness is now a rarity in the NBA.

John Stockton would make his return and season debut on December 8, 1997, just as the Jazz were rolling even without their starting point guard. Of course, Utah was even better with Stockton in the lineup though they had learned to play with Karl Malone initiating the plays. In the first 20 games that Stockton played after returning, the Jazz were 15-5, and the point guard averaged 12.7 points and 78 assists in limited performances.

But John Stockton would get back on track. He would help Utah win seven consecutive games in February of 1998. It started when he had 17 points, 18 assists, and five steals in a win over the Chicago Bulls on February 4 in a rematch of their Finals affair. During that run, he would average 11.6 points, 9.9 assists, and 2.7 steals. Overall, the Jazz would only lose two games in the 12 outings that John Stockton appeared in that month.

After failing to make the All-Star Game for the very first time since 1989, John Stockton still had enough star power in him to pull off some great throwback performances since the Utah Jazz were still leading the West. His best performance that season was when he helped defeat the New York Knicks on March 22. Stockton had 22 points, 14 assists, and three steals that night.

At 36 years old and at after missing 18 games during the regular season, John Stockton averaged 12 points and 8.5 assists for a Utah Jazz team that won 62 games that year. That was the first time since 1988 that John Stockton was unable to average a double-double, though he was still regarded as one of the best point guards in the league especially since he was playing for one of the top teams.

The Utah Jazz would go on to face the Houston Rockets in the first round in what was a rematch of their Western Conference Finals of last year. In what was a hard-fought series, the Rockets gave the Jazz a scare after winning Games 1 and 3 to lead 2-1. However, the Utah Jazz proved that they were championship contenders by winning Games 4 and 5 in blowout fashion to proceed to the second round. Stockton's best performance was in Game 2 when he had 17 points, ten assists, and four steals.

The highlight of the Jazz's second-round matchup with the San Antonio Spurs was Karl Malone's battle with standout rookie Tim Duncan in a fight between the past and future of the power forward position. Though the attention was all on Malone and Duncan, Stockton quietly contributed to winning Games 1 and 2 after posting a combined effort of 32 points and 20 assists in those two outings.

While the Jazz may have won the first two games to lead the series 2-0, the San Antonio Spurs fought back to win Game 3 by 22 points. Nevertheless, experience and chemistry won and the Utah Jazz went on to win the series despite the mediocre performances that John Stockton put up in those final two games. For a second consecutive season, the Jazz would proceed to the Western Conference Finals by beating the Spurs in five games.

Facing a vastly-improved Laker team headlined by All-Star duo Shaquille O'Neal and Kobe Bryant, the Utah Jazz were in for a tough fight against a 61-win squad. However, that was not the case as the Jazz defeated the Lakers in Game 1 by 35 points. That blowout win in Game 1 was the theme of what was a quick series the Utah Jazz, who defeated the Los Angeles Lakers in four games thanks to their experience and sheer determination to get back to the NBA Finals.

That quick four-game sweep was supposed to benefit an old veteran team like the Utah Jazz, who relied on the Stockton and Malone combo, who were both past age 35 at that time. They had a total of ten days of rest before the NBA Finals, where they were about to face the Chicago Bulls in a rematch of last year's Finals. However, the Jazz were the favorites in that series. They were both 62-win teams but Utah defeated Chicago in both of their meetings during the regular season. And what was supposed to spell the difference was that the Jazz had an extended rest before the NBA Finals while the Bulls fought a hard-fought seven-game series against the Indiana Pacers.

A well-rested John Stockton would show up in Game 1 of the NBA Finals. He made 9 of his 12 field goal attempts to score 24 points in addition to dishing out eight assists in that overtime win over a Bulls team that did not seem weary from their battle with the Pacers. However, Chicago proved that they were the defending champions by going for a win in Game 2 while John Stockton struggled to produce in that bout.

As the series moved to Chicago for Games 3 to 5, the Bulls had an opportunity to win the championship on their home floor. The Utah Jazz seemed lethargic after scoring only 54 points in Game 3 while the Bulls took the series lead from them. But while the Jazz may have performed marginally better in Game 4 where John Stockton had seven points and a playoff high of 13 assists, the Chicago Bulls still won that close bout to go up 3-1 in the series.

John Stockton would go for six points, 12 assists, and five steals in Game 5 to help the Utah Jazz push the series back to Utah for Game 6 and 7, where they had an opportunity to win the championship on their home floor. And in Game 6, they even had a chance to force Game 7 considering that they had the lead in the final seconds of the game. It was John Stockton that nearly iced the game after hitting a three-pointer that gave the Utah Jazz a slim 86-83 lead with 42 ticks left on the clock. But then Michael Jordan happened.

The circumstances were similar to last season's. Jordan secured possession after stealing the ball right after making a layup that tied the game. But this time, the Bulls could not draw up a play and Jordan would not pass the ball out to Kerr. He was going to take it by himself. Going up against Byron Russell, the Utah Jazz's best perimeter defender, MJ dribbled right and stepped back with a crossover while seemingly warding off his man with his right arm and rose up for a 20-foot jump shot that gave the Bulls a one-point lead with five seconds left.

The series once again seemed to have been iced from a Michael Jordan play, and the Utah Jazz would fail to convert over at the other end when John Stockton missed a three-pointer that would have forced Game 7. For a second straight season, Jordan was the figure that denied his fellow 1984 draft classmate John Stockton from an NBA title. And unfortunately for Stockton, that would be the final time he would have a chance at a championship. Karl Malone would later have one more shot when he joined the Lakers in the 2003-04 season. As for John Stockton, that was his last hurrah especially since he was not getting any younger.

The Steady Decline

Shortly after the Chicago Bulls won the 1998 championship, Michael Jordan would retire from basketball for the second time in his career. And after everything from the 1997-98 season had concluded, a labor dispute between the owners and players' association led to a long lockout which delayed the start of the NBA season. It was not until February of 1999 that the NBA would resume operations.

The long rest benefitted an old team like the Utah Jazz, who were relying on a 36-year-old John Stockton and a 35-year-old Karl Malone. But even though the duo were already aging deep into their 30's, they still proved to be able to match up with the younger players. On Stockton's part, it was his longevity and durability that made him legendary among players. Though he was a few weeks shy of age 37, he still played and moved like he was 27.

The Utah Jazz, who were still focused on winning a title even after losing in the NBA Finals twice in a row, would start the shortened 50-game season hot by winning six consecutive games. Stockton's best performance during that run was in that second win, which was versus the Lakers on February 7. He had 26 points and 11 assists that night. And in that sixth straight win, John Stockton went for ten points and 15 assists.

While John Stockton may have still been better than perhaps 90% of all the other point guards in the league even at his age, what was evident was that he was on the decline. Double-digit assists games became a rarity for him that season and he would only go over ten assists 13 times. He only had nine double-doubles in 50 games of action.

But even though John Stockton was slowing down, the Utah Jazz did not seem like they had given up on their hope of making it back to the NBA Finals after they won 37 games during the regular season. Karl Malone was even named league MVP for a second time in his career at his advanced age. It was clear that the Stockton and Malone pick-and-roll duo was still effective despite the aging core.

Now in his 15th season in the NBA, John Stockton averaged 11.1 points and 7.5 assists in 28 minutes of action. He played all 50 games that season and averaged the lowest numbers he had since breaking out during the 1987-88 season. Father Time was finally catching up, though Stockton's durability and stamina were already impressive even at his age.

An aging Utah Jazz would face a younger and faster Sacramento Kings squad in the first round of the playoffs. John Stockton would match up with a young Jason Williams, a point guard that might not have become a star but was capable of putting on shows because of his flashy style of passing. The 37-year-old John Stockton was out there to prove that even his old school style would outplay Williams' flashiness, which was a stark contrast to how the older point guard did things.

Though the Jazz started things off with a 30-point win in Game 1, the Kings would use their speed and youth to run Utah into the ground and to take a 2-1 series lead heading into Game 4. However, experience eventually won out. The Utah Jazz would use their grit and veteran smarts to outplay the Kings in Games 4 and 5 to make it to the second round. Stockton had 12 points and 14 assists in that closeout game.

Unfortunately for the Utah Jazz, a younger and equally gritty Portland Trailblazers had their number in the second round. While John Stockton had throwback performances at certain points in that series, it was not enough. The Trailblazers ousted the defending Western Conference champions in six games to deny the Gonzaga product of a chance at a title once again.

While John Stockton may have been one of the elder statesmen in the NBA, he still had a lot of throwback performances during the 1999-2000 season on his way to becoming one of the few players to play in three different decades. He would have six double-double performances in his first 20 games of the season. His best output at that early juncture was when he had 18 points and 12 assists in a win over the Milwaukee Bucks on November 20, 1999.

On January 3, 2000, John Stockton would have a season high of 18 assists on top of the 12 points he had in a win over the Denver Nuggets. But more than two weeks after that, he would have a performance that made him look like he was ten years younger. In a loss to the Minnesota Timberwolves on January 19, Stockton would go for 23 points and 12 assists. He would have four consecutive double-digit assists games after that. And in one of those games, he had 22 points and 13 assists in a win over the Sacramento Kings.

With John Stockton performing a lot better than his age would tell, he was named as a member of the Western Conference All-Stars for a tenth and final time in his long and storied career. He and Karl Malone were the only ones to have at least ten All-Star appearances on that roster since most of the other selections were youngsters that were set to lead the league into the new millennium. Stockton had ten points and two assists that night.

Proving that he and the Utah Jazz were still one of the most effective teams in the NBA, John Stockton would lead his team to a nine-game streak early in March. He had several throwback performances during that run. He would score 22 versus the Charlotte Hornets on March 3 and then had 18 assists against the Cleveland Cavaliers in their fifth straight win.

After that win streak ended, John Stockton would go for five more double-digit assist games in the Jazz's final 18 games of the season. He scored at least 20 points twice in that span of games. His best passing night in those final 18 games was when he had 14 assists on top of 16 points and five steals in a loss to the Dallas Mavericks on March 27.

In season number 16 for John Stockton, the ten-time All-Star point guard and league's all-time assists leader would average 12.1 points, 8.6 assists, and 1.7 steals as he proved that he was not ready to retire from basketball. He would also lead the Utah Jazz, who were still title contenders, to 55 wins during the regular season. For the 16th straight season since getting drafted by the Jazz, Stockton was headed to the playoffs.

John Stockton and Gary Payton would renew their rivalry in the first round of the playoffs when the Utah Jazz met the Seattle SuperSonics. Facing one of his rivals at the point guard spot in the 90's, John Stockton seemed like a younger man in that series. He would have ten points and ten assists to lead the Jazz to a win in Game 1. He would then go for 21 points and 11 assists in a 14-point Game 2 win.

While the Sonics may have evened the series up by winning Games 3 and 4 by double digits, John Stockton was at his best in Game 5. The All-Star point guard would go for 17 points, seven rebounds, and 15 assists to lead the Utah Jazz to the second round for another chance at making a deep playoff run. Stockton had double-digit assists in all five of those games and averaged 13 points and 12.2 dimes in that first-round win against the Sonics.

Unfortunately for the Utah Jazz, they would once again meet the Portland Trailblazers. While the Blazers may have had the Jazz's number the last season, they were also able to acquire a new player that also had Utah's number, especially during the 1997 and 1998 NBA Finals. Scottie Pippen would help lead the Blazers to a five-game win over the Jazz, who would lose three consecutive games by double digits before barely preventing a sweep in Game 4. For a second straight season, the Jazz were denied another deep playoff run by losing in the second round.

A 38-year-old John Stockton looked like he was 28 years old at the start of the 2000-01 season when he went for two great double-double performances in wins over the LA Clippers and the LA Lakers. Against the Clips, he had 11 points and 14 assists. And when he helped defeat the defending champions, John Stockton had 21 points and 14 assists. He would then help lead Utah to a 5-0 start by averaging 14 points and 10.8 assists during that run.

Not one to give way to the younger point guards of the NBA, John Stockton would go for four straight double-double performances from December 2 to 9 of 2000. He was averaging 12.3 points and 12.5 assists during that run. And two weeks later, he would go for his best double-double performance at that early part of the season. He would go for 19 points and 12 assists in that loss to the Philadelphia 76ers.

On January 13, 2001, John Stockton would go for his second 20-10 game of the season when he went for 21 points, five rebounds, and 11 assists in a win over the Los Angeles Lakers. That was the second time that season that Stockton had at least 20 points and ten assists in a win over the defending champions of the NBA. That was also the final time he would have a 20-10 performance that season.

While John Stockton would not have another 20-10 game that season, he was close to those numbers on numerous ocassions. He had 20 points and eight assists in a win in Sacramento on February 18. Then on March 5, Stockton had a new season-high of 22 points in addition to eight assists in a win over the Atlanta Hawks while playing only 29 minutes that night. Stockton would score over 20 points for the final time that season on April 15 when he finished a loss to the Timberwolves with 21 points and seven assists.

At the conclusion of the 2000-01 regular season, John Stockton averaged 11.5 points and 8.7 assists. He shot 50.4% from the floor that season despite the fact that he turned 39 years old that season and was a 6'1" point guard that played out on the perimeter. And even though he and Malone were closer to 40 than they were to 35, the Utah Jazz were still able to make the playoffs with a 53-win record.

However, it had become evident that the Utah Jazz no longer had enough gas in the tank to make a deep playoff run for another chance at the NBA title. After the Jazz won Games 1 and 2 of their first-round series against the Dallas Mavericks, the younger inside-outside power forward and point guard duo eventually triumphed. Dirk Nowitzki, who would soon become one of the best power forwards in the game, and Steve Nash, who would soon become the best passing point guard in the league, would outplay their older legendary counterparts in the final three games of the series. The Utah Jazz would bow out of the playoffs in the first round.

While Stockton may have already accepted that he may not make it back to the Finals especially since new young stars were taking over the NBA, he still put up excellent performances during the 2001-02 season. He had 18 points and 14 assists in the Jazz loss on opening night on October 30, 2001. And after that loss, he would have 19 points and 11 assists in a losing effort against the Lakers two nights later. Jon Stockton would have a season-high in assists on November 16 after going for 17 assists in addition to the eight points he scored in a win over the Washington Wizards, who featured a returning Michael Jordan.

But Stockton's best performance that season was yet to come. He would go for 21 points and 12 assists in a win over the Dallas Mavericks on December 10. He would then go for his second 20-10 game of the season on December 27 when he had 20 points and 11 assists in the Utah Jazz's win over the Portland Trailblazers, the team that eliminated them twice in the last three playoffs.

It was on January 19, 2002, when John Stockton had his season-high in points. In that loss to the Dallas Mavericks, he would go for 24 points, nine assists, and three steals to barely miss a 20-10 performance. On February 15, he would come close to that output once again after going for 23 points and ix assists in a win over the Toronto Raptors.

But Stockton would exceed those numbers near the end of the season. He would go for 26 points on 7 out of 11 shooting from the floor and 12 out of 12 form the free throw line in a win over the Golden State Warriors on April 13. And in the last game of the regular season, he would go for his third 20-10 game that year after finishing with 23 points and ten assists.

At the end of the season, John Stockton was averaging 13.4 points, 8.2 assists, and 1.9 steals. He also shot 51.7% from the floor as a 40-year-old point guard that was putting up numbers that not even 20-year-old rookies could. On top of playing all 82 games while averaging 31 minutes a night, Stockton's durability and stamina put a lot of the younger point guards in the NBA to shame. He would help lead the Jazz to 44 wins to make the playoffs for an 18th straight season since he was drafted by the same franchise in 1984.

Unfortunately for John Stockton, neither he nor the Utah Jazz had enough left in the tank to compete against younger and faster teams in the playoffs. They would lose to the Sacramento Kings in four games in their first-round matchup. That loss to the higher-seeded team signaled the end of the Jazz's years as one of the better playoff contenders in the West. It also showed that Stockton's years in the NBA were numbered.

The Final Season, Retirement

At 40 years old, John Stockton still looked like the towel boy that shocked everyone when he was drafted by the Utah Jazz in the first round of the 1984 NBA Draft. However, at that point, he was already at the tail end of his career as he entered his 19th season in the league. But even though he was the oldest player in the league at that time, he was still playing better than even the youngest point guards in the NBA.

One indication of Stockton's ability to still put up throwback numbers was when he had 22 point, ten assists, and four steals on December 2, 2002, in a win over the Indiana Pacers. About a month later on January 3, 2003, he would go for 20 points, five rebounds, eight assists, and three steals in a win over the Milwaukee Bucks. But seventeen days later, he proved himself as a capable scorer at any given moment by going for 25 points in a win over the New Jersey Nets.

John Stockton would go for his second 20-10 game that season when he had 20 points and ten assists in a loss to the Sacramento Kings on March 7. He would finish the final 21 games of the season with six double-digit assist games and three double-double performances. And when he finished the season, he was already 41 years old and was the seventh-oldest player to play in the NBA.

At 41 years old, John Stockton was averaging 10.8 points, 7.7 assists, and 1.7 steals in 28 minutes of action and while playing all 82 games of the regular season. Even at his advanced age, there was no rest for one of the NBA's best iron men. But that turned out to be the final 82-game marathon he would ever play. The 47-win Jazz would not even last long against the Sacramento Kings in the 2003 playoffs.

After bowing out of the playoffs, John Stockton announced that he had already played his final NBA game. On May 3, 2003, the 41-year-old ten-time All-Star made his retirement from the game of basketball official in a press release. He acknowledged the fact that he was still capable of playing more games but realized that, at his age, he already needed to spend more time with his growing family than to wait for games far away from his wife and children.[x]

The Utah Jazz would hold a retirement ceremony for him shortly after he announced his retirement. In customary John Stockton fashion, the ten-time All-Star would attend the ceremony dressed as a simple man that did not revel in the cheers and adoration of the crowd. He still had his usual stoic game face on while the people of Salt Lake City cheered him on.

As stoic as Stockton seemed, tears suddenly began to roll down his face when his coach Jerry Sloan began talking. After the city mayor announced that the street in front of the Jazz's arena would be named Stockton Drive, Sloan was emotional in saying that there was no other player in the league that had the body of work that his point guard had. Saying that he thought that the ten-time All-Star was going to stay with him and the Jazz forever, Sloan recognized that he and John Stockton had a wonderful run together in the 19 years he played for the franchise.[xi]

Karl Malone was the next to make John Stockton emotional. The man that has been his partner since 1985 and the player responsible for finishing half of his assists in a partnership that lasted for 18 years was more than just his teammate, but a family member. Malone said that Stockton taught him more about life than he did about basketball.[xi] This was coming from a man that had become the omega to Stockton's alpha. It was a partnership that could not have lasted had any one of those players were been selfish. But both Stockton and Malone complemented each other's game and personality. Sadly, it was the end of what is arguably one of the best partnerships in league history.

John Stockton would end his career as a member of the Utah Jazz after 19 years. At that time, he owned the record for most seasons playing for one franchise until Kobe Bryant broke it in 2016. Stockton also finished his career with 15,806 career assists. He was more than 5,000 assists ahead of the man next to him. He also retired as the league's all-time leader in career steals after recording 3,265. He was more than 700 steals ahead of Michael Jordan in that regard.

But more than the records he broke and owned, John Stockton retired as the best passing point guard and one of the most durable players in the history of the NBA. While some would say that Magic Johnson is the best point guard in league history, Stockton may have owned that distinction had he won at least one NBA title. Championships may help define a player's place as one of the all-time greats but it was the way John Stockton turned heads around, proved everyone wrong, and made winning plays in his 19 seasons as an NBA player that made him one of the best players in league history.

Chapter 4: International Career

John Stockton was not only dishing dimes in the NBA but was also one of the nation's most crucial players in their two Olympic gold medal wins in 1992 and 1996. While he may have missed Bob Knight's 1984 Olympic squad, there was no doubt that he had developed into the league's best passing point guard when he was named in a member of the 1992 Dream Team, the first USA Olympic Basketball Team that featured NBA players.

While the rest of the world was more focused on Michael Jordan, Larry Bird, Magic Johnson, and Charles Barkley during the 1992 Olympics in Barcelona, Spain, John Stockton was a silent worker for the team. He would only play four games the entire tournament to average 2.8 points and two assists for an unbeatable US squad that easily won the gold medal.

John Stockton would return to the Olympics in 1996 together with returnees such as teammate Karl Malone, Scottie Pippen, and Charles Barkley. Playing in all eight games of the tournament, which was held in Atlanta, USA, Stockton would once again help win the gold medal in easy fashion. He averaged 3.8 points and 2.8 assists as the third point guard playing behind Gary Payton and Penny Hardaway.

Hall of Fame Induction

In April 2009, John Stockton was chosen as one of the headliners to be named as a member of the Naismith Basketball Hall of Fame. He and his head coach Jerry Sloan were selected to be inducted into the Hall of Fame the same year. Stockton and Sloan joined a star-studded cast that included San Antonio Spurs great David Robinson and Michael Jordan, arguably the best player in league history.

Though the spotlight was on Michael Jordan, John Stockton turned heads when he selected Isiah Thomas to introduce him into the Hall of Fame. The Utah Jazz and Detroit Pistons of the 80's were never the best of friends. The same could be said about Stockton and Thomas, who was rumored to have been bitter that the former was chosen over him to play in the 1992 Olympics.

However, Isiah Thomas could not have said better words to describe John Stockton when he introduced the ten-time All-Star into the Hall of Fame. He said that Stockton was the person that embodied the point guard position because he knew everything he needed to do. He knew when it was the right time for him to score and when he needed to make the right pass.[xii] It was a fitting description from one Hall of Fame point guard to another.

During his induction speech, John Stockton was the first to say that he felt like he did not belong to the Hall of Fame but still recognized that he was one of the most competitive basketball players for a total of 30 years. But he never talked too much about himself and instead took time to recognize the people that have supported him ever since he was a little kid playing in Spokane, Washington. But the highlight of his speech was the joke he made about how Michael Jordan suddenly became cool just because he made a big shot. But other than that, Stockton's speech was all about the other guys that helped him get to the Hall of Fame.[xiii] It was befitting of a point guard that spent a 19-year NBA career making passes to others.

Chapter 5: Personal Life

John Stockton is married to Nada Stepovich, who is of Serbian descent. The two married back in 1986 when Stockton was still a few years fresh out of Gonzaga. Since then, they resided in Salt Lake City in Utah but have relocated to Stockton's hometown of Spokane, Washington when the All-Star point guard was nearing the end of his career.

Together, the Stockton couple has six children. Their two daughters are named Lindsay and Laura. Meanwhile, their sons are named Houston, Michael, David, and Samuel. Houston played college football instead of basketball and was a defensive back for the University of Montana. Meanwhile, both Michael and David play basketball. Michael attended Westminster College in Salt Lake City and would later play for two basketball teams in Germany. David, on the other hand, followed his father's footsteps in Gonzaga University and played for the D-League's Reno Bighorns after leaving college in 2014. He would then play for the Sacramento Kings in 2015 for one season. John's youngest, Laura Stockton, now also plays for Gonzaga.

Since retiring from basketball, John Stockton has led a quiet and simple life away from the spotlight and cameras. He would spend his early retirement years as an assistant coach for several youth teams all at once. He has also spent time developing some of Utah Jazz's point guards, which includes his heir-apparent, Deron Williams.

In 2015, after he was not selected to replace Ty Corbin as the Utah Jazz's next head coach, John Stockton joined Montana State University as an assistant coach for its women's basketball team. He was selected as an assistant because of his experience as a coach of several of the team's players when he was coaching for teams in the AAU leagues.

John Stockton and Karl Malone have always been good friends and have kept in contact with one another even after they retired from basketball. Throughout their career as a duo, they would go everywhere as a pair. They dined together at each other's houses and Stockton has also learned how to pass the chicken to Malone just as well as he passed the ball to him on the pick-and-roll. It was a relationship that has transcended past the pick-and-roll and basketball court.

Jerry Sloan has also become one of John Stockton's closest friends. Sloan was one of the very reasons for Stockton's success as the former trusted him with the pick-and-roll. But Jerry Sloan was quick to say that Stockton was the reason he was the Utah Jazz's coach for so long. It was a partnership that started in 1985 when Stockton was still fresh off his rookie season and Sloan was still an assistant. It lasted for 18 seasons until John Stockton retired. The partnership stayed strong as both of them shared the stage when they were inducted into the Hall of Fame at the same time.

Chapter 6: Impact on Basketball and Legacy

John Stockton's impact on the game of basketball has always been how he revolutionized the position and role of being a pure passing point guard. While the league has seen its share of pass-first point guards such as Bob Cousy and Magic Johnson, none of them were able to do so much in their career just by being a passer. Cousy may have been the orchestrator of the 50's Boston Celtics while Magic may have been the cog that got the Showtime Lakers of the 80's moving, none of them made passing as much of an art as Stockton did.

Described as the perfect point guard, John Stockton knew when to score when he needed to and when to make the right plays at the right time. He was always an exceptional decision-maker because of the way he controlled the point guard position like no other playmaker in league history has ever done. And he did so in a career that spanned two decades.

Stockton knew his place and his spots as he averaged 51.5% from the floor as a scorer. He never took bad shots and always made sure he would make the ones he attempted. It did not matter where he was shooting because everything he attempted almost always seemed like the best shots available for him. That was the very reason why he led the league in field goal percentage among guards for several seasons.

As good of a decision-maker as he was when he was trying to score, Stockton was even better at making decisions as a passer. He rarely turned the ball over when trying to make plays for his teammates. John Stockton always knew when to make passes and where to find his teammates for open shots. He made everyone on the team look good because of the way he controlled the tempo and pace of the game as a passer. His fantastic ability to make decisions and passes was the very reason he was able to lead the league in assists for a record nine consecutive seasons.

However, arguably his biggest impact as a revolutionary point guard was how he made the pick-and-roll basketball's most unstoppable play during his time with the Utah Jazz. He was the maestro that got the pick-and-roll going while the rest of his teammates were waiting for him to find them. Some would argue that Karl Malone was the reason for the pick-and-roll's success but it was how John Stockton was able to orchestrate basketball's most basic play that made it such a huge success. He was the alpha while Malone was the omega.

With John Stockton initiating the pick-and-roll, there was no stopping the Jazz from scoring. When the screen was set, Stockton would almost usually find a rolling or open Karl Malone for an easy basket. And if defenses keyed in on Malone, Stockton had other options especially since the floor was wide open for him to make passes to his other teammates. And whenever he did not have an option for the pass, John Stockton could take the ball all the way to the basket or could get to his spots for open shots. It all seemed too basic and elementary but Stockton made something so simple into the most dangerous play in basketball because of his transcendent abilities as a passer and as a decision-maker.

Stockton's ability to run the pick-and-roll as an all-time great pass-first point guard became the prototype for a lot of future point guards and teams. Steve Nash, shortly after Stockton's retirement, became known for his ability to run the pick-and-roll in Phoenix with Amar'e Stoudemire. Deron Williams, Utah's next great point guard after Stockton, ran that same play under Jerry Sloan almost to perfection even though his power forward Carlos Boozer did not have the same finishing abilities as Karl Malone did. Chris Paul, during his time with the New Orleans Hornets and the Los Angeles Clippers, also run the pick-and-roll effectively. All those point guards were able to achieve double-digit assists in several seasons precisely because of how Stockton changed the way the pick-and-roll was being played.

As for the Utah Jazz, one of the biggest impacts that John Stockton had on that team was how he made it relevant. From 1984 to 2003, Stockton made the playoffs in all of his years as a player as one of the key figures of that Utah Jazz roster. The Jazz were always a small market team that struggled to make it big in the NBA even when Pete Maravich and Adrian Dantley were there. However, it was during Stockton's time as a duo with Karl Malone that the Jazz saw consistency.

John Stockton, in a lot of ways, was a reflection of Utah. He was simple, soft-spoken, and stoic. But underneath it all was the heart of a lion that worked harder than anyone else. That was the reason why he was so beloved by the people of Salt Lake City. Not only did he turn the franchise around to become of the NBA's most consistent teams during his time but he was also able to become the very embodiment of the hardworking Utah Jazz team. With that, perhaps no other player has had the impact on his position and on his team at the same time than John Stockton has had.

Because of John Stockton, the pass-first point guard has become a norm in today's NBA. Steve Nash, the player that resembled him the most, followed him as the NBA's best pure point guard for several seasons. He also ran the pick-and-roll just as great as Stockton did. Following Nash were Deron Williams and Chris Paul. Williams and big man Carlos Boozer were the incarnation of the Stockton and Malone tandem though they did not last that long. Meanwhile, Chris Paul made a career out of being the NBA's best pure point guard during his peak. He made passing an art form just like Stockton did. He would lead the NBA in assists six times, which is just three short of John Stockton's achievement.

John Stockton's legacy as a pass-first point guard has gone on to live with the next generation of unselfish playmakers that would always make it a point to pass the ball first than to score it. No other player in league history has found more happiness in seeing his teammates score the ball than Stockton did. However, today's NBA players have slowly been learning from his example as the league has trended towards an unselfish style of play that focuses more on ball movement. Had Stockton played in today's era, he would have surely been one of the most successful point guards, especially because of his toughness, shooting, and playmaking skills.

Some would say that the biggest knock on John Stockton's status as one of the all-time greats is that he was unable to win a title in the 18 years he played in the league. However, he could not be blamed for such when he was playing at a time when the league was at its most competitive in recent memory and when Michael Jordan and the Chicago Bulls were dominating the NBA. And if anybody were to question his status as one of the best to have ever played the sport, his accomplishments say it all.

Leading the league in all-time assists by more than 3,000 dimes more than the next guy, finishing his career as the all-time steals leader by a large margin, appearing in 10 All-Star Games, nominated to the All-NBA and All-Defensive Teams at a combined 16 times, getting named as one of the 50 Greatest Players of All Time in 1996, and making it to the basketball Hall of Fame, John Stockton has done everything a player could ever dream of even though he never won a title. There was never a knock on how great he was when you look at his body of work and accomplishments in the NBA.

And while he may be considered one of the best players to never win a championship, the better description for him is that he is one of the best revolutionaries in NBA history. A winner, game-changer, model athlete, ideal teammate, and hard-working leader, John Stockton's accomplishments and contributions to basketball can never be duplicated. And when you look at his body of work over a span of 19 seasons in the NBA, the only conclusion one can come to is that there can never be another point guard of John Stockton's caliber.

Final Word/About the Author

I was born and raised in Norwalk, Connecticut. Growing up, I could often be found spending many nights watching basketball, soccer, and football matches with my father in the family living room. I love sports and everything that sports can embody. I believe that sports are one of most genuine forms of competition, heart, and determination. I write my works to learn more about influential athletes in the hopes that from my writing, you the reader can walk away inspired to put in an equal if not greater amount of hard work and perseverance to pursue your goals. If you enjoyed *John Stockton: The Inspiring Story of One of Basketball's Greatest Point Guards*, please leave a review! Also, you can read more of my works on *Roger Federer, Novak Djokovic, Andrew Luck, Rob Gronkowski, Brett Favre, Calvin Johnson, Drew Brees, J.J. Watt, Colin Kaepernick, Aaron Rodgers, Peyton Manning, Tom Brady, Russell Wilson, Michael Jordan, LeBron James, Kyrie Irving, Klay Thompson, Stephen Curry, Kevin Durant, Russell Westbrook, Anthony Davis, Chris Paul, Blake Griffin, Kobe Bryant, Joakim Noah, Scottie Pippen, Carmelo Anthony, Kevin Love, Grant Hill, Tracy McGrady, Vince Carter, Patrick Ewing, Karl Malone, Tony Parker, Allen Iverson, Hakeem Olajuwon, Reggie Miller, Michael Carter-Williams, John Wall, James Harden, Tim Duncan, Steve Nash,*

Draymond Green, Kawhi Leonard, Dwyane Wade, Ray Allen, Pau Gasol, Dirk Nowitzki, Jimmy Butler, Paul Pierce, Manu Ginobili, Pete Maravich, Larry Bird, Kyle Lowry, Jason Kidd, David Robinson, LaMarcus Aldridge, Derrick Rose, Paul George, Kevin Garnett, Chris Paul, Marc Gasol, Yao Ming, Al Horford, Amar'e Stoudemire, DeMar DeRozan, Isaiah Thomas, Kemba Walker and Chris Bosh in the Kindle Store. If you love basketball, check out my website at claytongeoffreys.com to join my exclusive list where I let you know about my latest books and give you lots of goodies.

Like what you read? Please leave a review!

I write because I love sharing the stories of influential athletes like John Stockton with fantastic readers like you. My readers inspire me to write more so please do not hesitate to let me know what you thought by leaving a review! If you love books on life, basketball, or productivity, check out my website at claytongeoffreys.com to join my exclusive list where I let you know about my latest books. Aside from being the first to hear about my latest releases, you can also download a free copy of *33 Life Lessons: Success Principles, Career Advice & Habits of Successful People*. See you there!

Clayton

References

[i] Rushin, Steve. "City of Stars". *Sports Illustrated.* 27 July 1992. Web.

[ii] McCallum. "Not a Passing Fancy". *Sports Illustrated.* 25 April 1988. Web.

[iii] Weaver, Dan (September 17, 1990). "Stockton: one of the NBA's premier point guards sweated his way to superstar status". *Spokesman Review.*

[iv] Goodwin, Dale (February 22, 1980). "Stockton: Slow to grow, quick to score". *Spokesman Review.*

[v] Hamilton, Linda. (June 20, 1984). "The more you see him, the more you like him". *Deseret News.*

[vi] Blackwell, Dave (June 20, 1984). "Stockton picked hailed as Jazz coup". *Deseret News.*

[vii] Merkin, Scott. "Green Glories in Run' n' gun". *Chicago Tribune.* 12 June 1998. Web.

[viii] Falk, Aaron. "How did Karl Malone fall to the Jazz in the 1985 draft?". *Salt Lake Tribune.* 25 June 2015. Web.

[ix] Goldaper, Sam. "Tripucka traded by Pistons for Dantley". *The New York Times.* 22 August 1986. Web.

[x] "John Stockton on Jordan, Malone and post-NBA life". *CNN.* 11 November 2013. Web.

[xi] Buckley, Tim. "The Long Goodbye". *Deseret News.* 8 June 2003. Web.

[xii] Genessy, Jody. "Utah Jazz: Stockton Chooses Isiah, Sloan picks Barkley as HOF presenters". *Deseret News.* 9 September 2002. Web.

[xiii] "Sloan, Stockton Hall of Fame acceptance speeches". *KSL.* 14 September 2009. Web.

Made in the USA
Coppell, TX
01 December 2022